Eleanor C. Donnelly

**A Klondike picnic**

The story of a day

Eleanor C. Donnelly

**A Klondike picnic**
*The story of a day*

ISBN/EAN: 9783742836700

Manufactured in Europe, USA, Canada, Australia, Japa

Cover: Foto ©Andreas Hilbeck / pixelio.de

Manufactured and distributed by brebook publishing software (www.brebook.com)

Eleanor C. Donnelly

**A Klondike picnic**

# A KLONDIKE PICNIC.

*THE STORY OF A DAY.*

BY

ELEANOR C. DONNELLY,

Author of "*Petronilla,*" "*Our Birthday Bouquet,*" etc.

WITH GENUINE LETTERS FROM TWO GOLD-SEEKERS

IN

ALASKA.

New York, Cincinnati, Chicago:
BENZIGER BROTHERS,
*Printers to the Holy Apostolic See.*
1898.

TO

THE DEAR DEVOTED MOTHER OF LEX AND LEE

THIS LITTLE BOOK IS DEDICATED,

BY THE AUTHOR.

# A KLONDIKE PICNIC.

## I.

It is a lovely morning in mid-May.

The sky is as blue as our Blessed Lady's cloak: and like fleecy bits of her white veil are the few small clouds floating here and there across the blue.

It has been a very backward spring—cold, and continuously wet. But the mercury has made a big jump in the night; and the sun, now barely up, shows a face as red as a scarlet rose—a sign, the old fisher-folk predict, of a proper hot day. The crickets, whirring like fairy mills in the salt grass, and the thin blue mists that steam over the meadows of Shell Beach, and out over the broad, dimpling ocean, somehow or other tell the same story.

Deliciously cool is the sea-breeze now, however. Yet one of the two women hurrying along the quiet street towards the railway station wipes her face with her handkerchief, while the other waves a big palm-leaf fan.

Joking and laughing as they go, they are plainly a pair of house-maids, off for a day's merry-making. They have fifteen minutes to make the morning express to Philadelphia.

On the terrace of the pretty cottage near the beach, which they have just quitted, two young ladies are poking about among the flower-beds.

Both blondes of a dainty and picturesque prettiness, the elder wears a spring gown of delicate lilac, the younger a blouse and skirt of blue flannel, embroidered by its wearer's little fingers with white silken daisies. Their eyes are as blue and clear as the waters of the sea, their cheeks as pink as the heart of the shells that lie upon its shore. Having thrown aside their garden hats, we see that their glossy hair is like sunshine, and fine as spun gold.

They wear gloves for their spring gardening. They have planted every flower there with their own little hands; and the growing and the blowing of the smallest bud is a matter of grave importance to them.

"Here's a white hyacinth just out!" cries the girl in lilac, bending a face as fair and sweet as the newcomer's over its cup.

"Here's another bud on my jonquil!" retorts the blue blouse from her corner; "and these daffodils and crocuses are sure to bloom before night!"

"Wouldn't a bunch of our violets be just the thing, sister, for the May-Queen's altar?" the first speaker is about to ask, when the cottage-door is flung noisily open, and a boy of thirteen clears the steps at a bound, shouting:

"O Veva! O Nan! Mother says we can have a picnic to the Klondike to-day!"

"*The Klondike?*" echoes Veva, looking up a little bewildered, and putting back the loose flakes of red-gold hair that fall about her pretty cheeks and ears.

She is seventeen, and something of a dreamer.

"Oh! I know!" cries Nan (two years her junior). "I heard Phil and the Winchester boys

8      A KLONDIKE PICNIC.

talking about it yesterday. It's the little rocky island out there beyond the bar, Veva," and she points seaward.

"Of course it is," grunts the boy, Philip; "and a dandy little spot, you bet!"

"But why on earth do you call it the *Klondike*, Phil?" questions Veva.

"Because it's full of rocks, don't you see? and full of—full of——"

"Gold?" laughs saucy Nan.

"Bother!" pouts Philip, "what do girls know about it? Anyhow, we've got our tent over there, and our mines, and all our traps; and Bert Winchester says if we can get as much gold out of it this year as you and Veva have got in your hair, he'll be satisfied!"

Nan's fair little face glows like a carnation, and Veva begins to laugh.

"Where are you off to now, Phil?" she asks, as the boy opens the gate, and runs away whistling down the street.

"Going to serve Mass, and tell Father Edwards about the picnic. He said he wanted to go with us the next time we went to the Klondike," shouts back her brother; and the silvery sound of a church-bell ringing far off in the village seems to punctuate his words.

"Veva," says Nan, "I'm afraid we won't be time enough for Mass."

"Girls!" cries a voice inside the cottage, "come help me get ready the lunch!"

The pretty young creatures find their mother at the big kitchen-table, spreading butter on a lot of thin slices of bread.

A dish of cold chicken, little jars of potted ham and tongue, pickles, cheese, biscuits, cake, pies, and a host of other "goodies" crowd the board.

Side by side, we see that Veva is her mother's radiant image. Both have tall, slender figures with a certain noble grace of motion; but the rich gold of Veva's hair has deepened in Mrs. Kirke's case into a dead brown, and the girl's brilliant complexion puts on a faded color in her mother's cheeks.

Nan is a bewitching fairy, not up to Veva's shoulder. There is something exquisite about her, as if made of finer clay than others. Her delicate skin, her flossy hair, her blue eyes are all several shades lighter than her sister's.

"Now, children," says Mrs. Kirke, "make ready the sandwiches. It's going to be dreadfully hot, I fear. But cook and Susan are off to the city for the day, and your father won't be here till the last train. Philip coaxed so hard for a picnic, I hadn't the heart to say no."

"Oh, well, momsie dear," laughs Nan, "we're going to the Klondike, anyway, and we ought to be able to keep cool *there*, if Cousin Lex and Cousin Lee are to be believed."

"By the way, will Aunt Grace come along?" asks V.eva, spreading the potted ham and mustard between the dainty little squares of bread.

"Philip is to stop and ask her after he sees Father Edwards. That dear little priest is as much of a boy as the rest of them," smiles the mother.

"I remember reading once," says Veva, with a grave look in her lovely, dark-blue eyes, "that men who are good and pure are always boys."

"Where do you preach next Sunday, sissie?" cries lively Nannie, rummaging in a near-by cupboard. "Here are the lunch-bags and boxes"—tumbling them out on the table. "If Phil wants to be a real Klondiker to-day, he must do all the 'packing' himself!"

"So he will, Miss Nan, and no thanks to you!" shouts a voice at her elbow that nearly costs the picnic the loss of a superb apple-pie; and there is Philip back again from his errands, red as a peony, and grinning from ear to ear.

"Speak of the angels," adds he, "and you'll hear the flapping of their wings. Father Edwards will go, and be glad, mother."

"Good, my son," returns Mrs. Kirke with a tender look at her only boy—her one ugly duckling, who is cross-eyed as well as red-haired. "And your Aunt Grace?"

"Has the headache, but will try to join us at lunch. Say, Veva," concludes Philip, munching a gingersnap, "put in plenty of stuff. The Winchester boys are coming, too."

"Mercy on us!" cries Nan, "all that hungry horde? It's well, sir, you are to do the 'packing' yourself. Go on inviting people at this rate, and it will take a camel to carry the lunch!"

"Or a jackass," laughs Philip; "and here" (he makes a low bow with his hand on his breast)—"here is one at your service, fair stingy-bones!"

> "How did you know him, my little dears?
> By his beautiful voice and his nice long ears."

sings Nan as she dances out of Philip's reach, and helps Veva and her mother fill the enormous baskets.

"Aunt Grace is worrying about Lex and Lee," murmurs Veva aside to Nan. "Oh, that dreadful Alaska! Lex's last letter in January told her they were on the trail again, going straight to the gold-fields. She hasn't had a line since."

"Horrible!" whispers Nan; "she doesn't know whether they are alive or dead!"

Philip puts his head between his sisters'.

"Talking secrets about Aunt Grace, eh? I told her to bring all the boys' Alaska letters when she comes this afternoon. The Winchester fellows are dying to hear them."

"What about the Winchester girls, Phil?" asks Veva, as she fastens the last shawl-strap. "Are they coming, too?"

"Jeannie and Olive said they would meet us on the car," replies Phil rather sheepishly: "and maybe their cousin, Miss Elliott—"

"Well, for pity's sake!" shrieks Nan; "is it a private picnic, or is it the *Charge of the Light Brigade?*"

"Have we enough to feed the Six Hundred?" queries Mrs. Kirke.

And, as the girls fly off to fetch their hats, Philip strikes an attitude, and begins to rant:

> "When can their glory fade?
> O the wild charge they made!
> All the world wonder'd.
> Honor the charge they made!
> Honor the Light Brigade—
> Noble six hundred!"

## II.

ALL hands are ready to board the little motor-car when it reaches the corner of the Kirke grounds.

It is an open summer car that runs hourly from the Inlet to Sand Peep, eight miles away.

There are not many people aboard. Philip helps in his mother and—the lunch.

A merry, girlish voice cries: "Here we are!" and Veva and Nan, climbing to a seat, are welcomed by two dark, pleasant-faced girls— one in scarlet organdie, the other in yellow— their wide straw hats trimmed with seaweeds.

These are Jeannie and Olive Winchester. Their next neighbor is an older girl—a simply-dressed girl with a sensible and what Philip calls an awfully jolly face.

Jeannie introduces her as "our cousin Margaret Elliott from Philadelphia"; and she and Nan and Olive are soon chattering gayly together, to Phil's intense relief. The matter of the lunch has weighed heavily on his mind; but he grins as he sees Veva nestle close to Jeannie Winchester, her own especial chum.

Both are thoughtful girls—much given to writing poetry on the sly, and hiding it from sight, as a chicken does her eggs.

The car-track runs alongside the ocean-front, and so close that all can see the blue waves breaking on the beach. The swift motion creates a delightful breeze.

"'What are the wild waves saying?'" asks Miss Elliott in the form of a conundrum.

"Come, take a bath!" cries Philip.

"Come, take a sail!" laughs Nan.

"Come, go to Europe!" murmurs Veva to Jeannie, who squeezes her arm with a wistful sigh. The friends cherish delicious dreams of an ocean voyage some day, and foreign travel.

"Wrong, all of you!" says Miss Elliott. "What else are 'the wild waves saying,' day and night, but—*Let us (s)pray!*"

"Water can't pray!" growls Phil, not seeing the point.

"Water *can* pray, my son,". corrects his mother. "How many of you remember Father Edwards' sermon last month?"

"Oh! yes," says Veva with a pretty gravity that becomes her sweet face. "You mean what he said on the Canticle of the Three Children in the Fiery Furnace?"

And then Jeannie and Olive begin to chant in concert (it was once an exercise at their convent commencement): "'Bless the Lord, ye fountains; seas and rivers, bless the Lord; whales and all that move in the waters, bless the Lord!'"

"The Psalmist also says," continues Mrs. Kirke: "'All ye waters that are above the heavens, bless the Lord. . . . Showers and dew, bless the Lord. . . . Dews and hoar frost, bless the Lord. . . . Ice and snow, bless the Lord!'"

"So you see, Master Bubby," cries Nan, "that water can make its devotions as well as the rest of creation. Liquid or solid, Philip, my boy, it can always say with truth: '*Let us (s-s-s-s)pray!*'" And drawing a tiny atomizer from her bag, she sends a puff of violet-water against her brother's freckled cheek.

"Give us another!" says he good-humoredly.

"Well, then, when did the men of Shell Beach work a miracle?"

"When they sold a lot!" snaps Phil spitefully.

It is an open secret that the Shell Beachers are just now languishing for a "boom."

"You mean boy! Have you nothing easier, Nannie darling?" pleads Olive with symptoms of mock-exhaustion.

"Give it up!" cry Veva and Jeannie.

"When they made *a board-walk!*" exclaims triumphant Nan.

In revenge, "Why is Nan like a caterpillar?" proposes Miss Elliott.

"Because she makes *the butter fly!*" comes from Nan herself. "Please, somebody, give us a harder one!"

"Why is Nan like an oyster?" asks Phil, one eye on his victim, and the other on the lunch-basket.

"Not because she is dumb?" suggests Olive slyly.

"Nor because she is fond of her bed?" asks Mrs. Kirke with a loving glance at her golden-haired Titania.

"Nit," says Phil, "but *because she can't climb a tree!*"

This reaching the height of the silly and ridiculous, the girls turn their backs on Master Kirke, and no one notices his next query: "Did you ever see *a horse fly?*"

"Sand Peep!" calls the conductor; and the car stops at the small station.

The Winchester boys in their outing flannels are drawn up in a line on the platform. They salute the ladies, soldier-fashion. They have come out on their wheels with Father Edwards—Herbert, Allen, Jack and Fred—all fine, manly lads, ranging from fourteen to eight.

The priest is young, almost boyish-looking, but very attractive. His face is refined and intelligent, and his pleasant manners make him a favorite with all. He is a shining light in the village of Shell Beach, because of his simple devotion to duty.

In sickness and trouble he visits Protestants and Catholics alike; and one afternoon each week he takes his tea with the Life-Guard at their post on the beach, leaving behind him many a sweet, strong word of wisdom for rough hearts to ponder over in the stormy night-watches of the coast.

Father Edwards combines, indeed, the innocence of the dove with the cunning of the serpent. His genial sympathy wins the confidence of the children. The boys are perfectly at home with him on all occasions.

Allen Winchester, having seen that the company's "bikes" are safely stored in a corner of the little station, now slides a square, flat book from under the priest's arm, asking: "What is this, Father?"

"A Klondike scrap-book," is the reply. "*My* contribution to the picnic."

"O Father!" cries Jack, "are you really going to read us some more nice bits about Alaska?"

"If I get the chance. But what is it, Philip?" as Master Kirke draws near with rather a downcast look.

"Nothing, sir; only Veva's brought her scrap-book, too, and how's a fellow to have any fun fishing or crabbing if it's just going to be dry reading out of books?"

"It won't be dry, Phil," whispers Herbert. "It's the best kind of sport to hear about that queer, wild place where the gold-mines are."

"Father Edwards has got the jolliest lot of clippings you ever saw," adds Jack. "But here's the boat, boys, and old Captain Saltee ready to take us off!"

"All aboard, ladies and gentlemen!" cries the Captain, a sunburned old sailor, who looks like a picture in his rough flannel suit, with his big straw hat and his broad bare feet. "In with your traps, young men, and take care of the ladies, God bless 'em!"

## III.

It is a merry party crowding into the Captain's sail-boat, which plies every hour (through the summer months) between Sand Peep and the Klondike. Certainly, to-day,

> "Youth is at the prow and pleasure at the helm."

"Make room for the minstrels!" shouts Herbert Winchester, and Olive with her mandolin and Jack with his mouth-organ are given seats of honor in the boat.

"Room for the commissary-general!" screams Philip, as he struggles on board, lugging the great basket of lunch and two or three boxes of candy.

"Strongest man in the world, eh, Kirke?" joke the boys. "Is it Sandow this time, or Phil McCool, the Irish giant?"

"It's Phil McCrosseye, the Jersey kid!" retorts Kirke, who is in high spirits, as he finds a dry corner for his stores, and relieves the strain of "packing" by pulling Nan's curls and tripping up little Fred.

Was there ever such a delicious sail?

It is now close to nine o'clock. The sea is like a mill-pond, and the south wind in their favor.

Old Saltee has such an easy time of it with the boat that he falls to telling funny coast-yarns, and queer stories of by-gone sails and sailors.

Oh, to think of the tremendous storms that he has weathered, and the gigantic fish that he has caught! There is even a thrilling ghost-story or two, which Father Edwards interrupts with a laughable account of his visit to the oyster-beds at Maurice Cove.

Miss Elliott then enchants them all with her experience of camp-life on a Mexican *rancho*.

The boys lay their heads together for a few minutes, plainly plotting mischief. There is some whispering, followed by some tittering and chuckling; then Philip straightens out his face, to ask demurely:

"Captain Saltee, have you ever been sick at sea?"

"Never!" cries old Saltee with seamanly pride.

"What, *never?*" shout all the boys in a breath.

Saltee has never heard of *Pinafore*. He tumbles innocently into the trap set for him by the madcaps.

"Well—hardly ever!" he owns up; and then he wonders where the fun is, and why everybody laughs—and why Philip rolls over, holding his sides, and even kicking his heels in a perfect gale of merriment.

Olive, pitying poor old Saltee's embarrassment, now tunes her mandolin, and Jack gives a flourish on his organ, and boys and girls both burst forth in an original chorus by Veva:

"The mermaids woo us with arms that wave
    Like foam on the billows free:
The siren chants, in her cool green cave,
    The song of the sunny sea.
Each breeze that sweeps o'er the sparkling main
    Is full of a healing balm;
The spray it brings is a blessèd rain,
    Tho' the sky be blue and calm.
        Yo ho, my lads, yo ho!

"Spurning the sands like a granite floor,
   To plunge in the breakers white—
Laugh, happy hearts, till the surges' roar
   Trembles with glad delight!
Now bending low to the curling wave,
   Now scatt'ring far and wide
Its glitt'ring drops, we gayly lave
   Our prow in the cooling tide.
              Yo ho, my lads, yo ho!

"Golden-bright as the best champagne,
   This fair, life-giving sea!
The old Greeks' cure for a heart in pain
   Was a bath in its waters free.
Dreamed they then of this strand of strands
   Whose breath one's being thrills?
An ocean bath on Shell Beach sands
   Hath cure for all our ills!
              Yo ho, my lads, yo ho!"

"Heaven bless their happy hearts!" murmurs Mrs. Kirke to Father Edwards; but before he can reply Phil shouts victoriously: "Land ahoy!" and rocky little Klondike pops up just ahead of the boat which, thanks to wise old Saltee's steering, swings safely round to the landing-steps.

There is a great deal of laughter and screaming among the girls as they scramble over the thwarts to the staircase, trying to keep their neat skirts and pretty little boots from wet or soil.

The boys are gallant young gentlemen, however, and do their part with a pleasant grace and good will.

"Such well-behaved lads are a real comfort," says Miss Elliott, as Herbert Winchester lands her safe and sound on the little wooden platform set in the rocks.

"There never were nicer boys than our boys of Shell Beach!" boasts Father Edwards with pardonable pride.

"How could they be anything else?" whispers Mrs. Kirke to Margaret. "They are with him half their time. He is too modest to suspect that they all take him for their model."

"Small wonder!" whispers back Miss Elliott. "He is simple and direct as a little child, yet his manners are charming. And this—" she cries, standing still and looking around her curiously—"this is really the Klondike of our dreams?"

"Yes," replies Herbert Winchester, making a low bow to the assembled company. "Ladies and gentlemen, you are now supposed to tread the soil of that famous spot

"'Where the gentle polar bear
Nips the trav'ller unaware;
And where, by day, they hunt the ermine,
But, by night, another vermin!'"

"For shame, Bert!" protest the girls. And, to cover Bert's blushes, "Here," cries Allen, running up to a large tent on a rocky terrace, with the Stars and Stripes floating above it, "here is Gold Dust Camp in the Skaguay Trail!"

"And over there," adds Jack, "are the Yukon River and Circle City and Dawson City."

"And down here beyond the camp," chirps Philip, pointing out several little round pools in a bit of salt marsh, "are Lake Tagish and Lake Bennett and Lake Linderman, clear out to the Stewart River, where Cousins Lee and Lex are going to strike it rich soon, and make us all millionaires."

There is a general laugh which almost drowns Herbert's question:

"Now, boys, what are we going to fly at first?"

"Let's mine!" shouts one.

"Fish!" cries another.

"Crab!" roars a third.

"Take a bath!" suggests a fourth.

"We can't mine to-day," grumbles Philip. "*That's* out of the question with all these girls along, poking their parasols into our pay-dirt!"

"Thank you, sir," says Nan with airy dignity. "This hot sun's beginning to blaze down on us, and we'll have better use for our parasols than poking their points into your old make-believe mines. Jack and Fred are going to take *us* fishing—aren't they, Olive?"

"Yes; and crabbing, too!" says Olive, setting her mandolin in a safe corner of the tent.

## IV.

It is really a very cosey camp.

The Winchester boys have had plenty of means to fit it out, and the Kirke homestead has given it many a treasure. There are rugs on the ground; a camp-table, lots of camp-chairs and stools, a couple of cots, a well-filled bookshelf (where Father Finn and Dr. Egan are largely in evidence); while the corners are crowded with balls and bats, crab-nets and fishing-poles, and a violin and banjo in their several cases.

Even the little Klondike stove for chilly days has not been omitted; and on the canvas wall hangs a parian statue of the Blessed Virgin with a holy-water shell at her feet.

This, the sweet guardian of the camp, was picked up on the rocks by Captain Saltee last winter and given to Father Edwards. It is all that remains of a vessel from France laden with statuary, that went to pieces thirty years ago on the treacherous shores of Sand Peep.

"Jack, Fred!" calls Father Edwards. "Some seats here for the ladies!" And the boys quickly carry out the camp-chairs to the shady side of the tent.

At the same moment Philip appears with the crab-nets and fishing-rods.

Nan, catching up a wicker creel, cries: "Come along, Olive! Come along, Jack, Fred and Phil! Let's try our luck over there on the Yukon River!"

"Won't the rest of you join us?" asks Jack politely. "We have plenty of nets and lines."

"I think Jeannie and I had better stay to help with the lunch," replies Veva, always considerate for her mother.

"How about Herbert and Allen?" questions Father Edwards, as those two young gentlemen throw themselves down on the sand at Mrs. Kirke's feet, using their straw hats as fans.

"Oh, *we* are to be the hewers of wood and

the drawers of water for the company!" reply Bert and Al.

Miss Elliott and Mrs. Kirke both protesting that it is getting too warm for dragging a line along a hot bank, the fisher lads and lassies go off to enjoy their sport, leaving the rest with Father Edwards to the cool comfort of a chat in the open.

"The chaplain of St. Aloysius-in-the-Mountains is with me just now," says the priest; "he asked to be left in charge of things at home to-day. He tells me that two of our Shell Beach girls won the medals at the convent for the prize-poems. I didn't need to ask him if the fortunate ones were Veva and Jeannie. Their happy faces showed it when they came home for the holidays."

Both girls blush, and cast down their eyes with becoming modesty.

"What was the theme, Veva?"

"It had to be something local, Father, and something drawn from nature. Jeannie chose the hill where the convent girls often go on pleasant afternoons to see the sun set."

"I happen to have a copy of the lines here," says Miss Elliott, drawing a paper from her bag. "Cousin Jeannie gave it to me this morning. I asked her for it. It well deserved the silver medal, *I* think."

"Please read it," says Mrs. Kirke; "none of us has heard it yet, except Veva."

"I will read it," retorts Margaret, avoiding Jeannie's pleading eyes, "on condition that you, in your turn, will read us Veva's verses. They are in the scrap-book I saw her slip into your bag on the boat."

"Capital!" shouts Allen.

"A fair bargain!" cries Herbert; and, in spite of the blushing protests of the two young poets, Miss Elliott rises to read with infinite taste:

*The Sunset Hill.*

The Sunset Hill! the Sunset Hill!
  How many joys are wound
Like shining coils about my heart
  With that familiar sound!

The pleasant steep, the balmy air,
  The softened light of eve—
Each happy voice and beaming eye
  Such dreamy mem'ries leave,

Of when we scaled the grassy slope
   With many a merry joke;
Our laughter, ringing up the hill,
   The sleeping echoes woke.

Oh, lighter hearts there could not be,
   Nor lighter steps, I ween,
Than throbbed upon that pleasant height
   Or trod its dewy green!

But jest and laughter both were hushed
   When, on the sunny hill,
We took our stand, and saw the land
   Grow shadowy and still—

Grow shadowy and still, with awe,
   As sank the glowing sun,
And all the myriad floating clouds
   Turned golden, one by one.

The dreamy sounds of insect life
   Fell thro' the twilight gray;
The tinkling bells of lowing kine
   That pawed their homeward way,

Came softly to the list'ning ear
   Upon the grassy steep,
As pleasant, soothing visions come
   To weary souls in sleep.

Across the landscape wide and still,
   In mingled light and shade,
E'en to the mountains blue and dim,
   Where amber vapors played,

Our eyes looked out in joy unspeeched,
   That near o'erflowed its fount;
A mist came o'er them as we gazed,
   That was not on the mount;

> The mist of grateful, happy tears
>   Which childhood's vision knows,
> When, on a mother's tender breast,
>   It breathes and calms its woes.
>
> So, Mother Nature, on thy breast
>   We dried our starting tears,
> And lo! the bliss of that brief rest
>   Must calm the woes of years.
>
> Dear days of joy that then went down!
>   O Sun that softly set!
> Ye were alike: ye came, ye went.
> Thanks to the God whose mercy sent!
>   Your glory haunts me yet.

A hearty clapping of hands greets the simple verses, imperfect as they are; but under cover of the mild excitement, Miss Veva is detected trying to steal away with her mother's bag.

Herbert and Allen promptly pounce upon the fair criminal, and after a gentle little scuffle rescue the bag and book from her slender grasp.

The poor young Sappho of Shell Beach pouts her pretty lips, and sits rubbing her rosy fingers ruefully as Mrs. Kirke puts on her glasses and proclaims the title of the gold-medal poem:

> *The Legend of Indian Spring.*
>
> There is a spot in the shadowy woods,
>   A beautiful, breezy spot
> Where the worn heart revels in solitude,
>   And the canker enters not.

The peace and the smile of God are there
    When the waves of sunlight flow
Thro' the parted boughs of the agèd trees
    To break on the bank below.

And a silver spring that an angel's hand
    Hath led from some ruder height,
Comes stealing down 'mid the fallen leaves
    To dance in the golden light.

Ages agone, in this forest home,
    The red men roamed and ruled;
And the callow youth of a mighty tribe
    To field and flood were schooled.

Lo! when the Indian race had waned,
    And the woods had ceased to ring
With the awful notes of the war-whoop wild—
    (The voice of a demon thing!),

The pallid shade of the fallen race
    (As ancient legends sing),
Toiled wearily down to this mystic place
    And died at the Indian Spring.

Oft, as I sit on the mossy bank,
    With the friends I love around,
The ancient legend wins my soul,
    And I hear a mournful sound—

The hollow groan of that tawny wraith
    Who saw his tribe decay,
And their treasured wealth of soil and stream
    Pass dreamily away.

And when these hours of joy are past,
    Perchance forever o'er,
And the sparkling drops of the dancing spring
    Shall visit my sight no more,

Still in my heart will a spring arise
   And wind its gentle way
'Mid the whisp'ring ferns of a memory fond
   Whose leaves will ne'er decay !

For the friendships formed at the Indian Spring,
   In the forest brown and hoar,
Shall live at the sparkling fount of thought
   Till Time shall be no more !

## V.

The applause that follows the poem is quite rapturous. All are amazed at the grace and beauty of the lines.

To hide her delighted confusion (for where is the authoress that is not moved by a general and cordial approval of her work?) Veva hastens to beg the young priest: "Please, Father, won't you give us something from your Klondike scrap-book? Every one likes to hear of that new, strange country."

Father Edwards gladly opens his well-filled book, and turns a number of pages with his slim, scholarly hand.

"Here," says he, at last, "is a romantic bit of word-painting which will please our household poets"—and he smiles at Veva and Jeannie. "I clipped it from a copy of the *Century*. It comes out of an article called 'The

Alaska Trip,' by John Muir, the naturalist. Mr. Muir says:

"'To the lover of wildness Alaska offers a glorious field for either work or rest: landscape beauty in a thousand forms, things great and small, novel and familiar, as wild and pure as Paradise. Wander where you may, wildness ever fresh and ever beautiful meets you in endless variety; ice-laden mountains, hundreds of miles of them, peaked and pinnacled and crowded together like trees in groves, and so high and so divinely clad in clouds and air that they seem to belong more to heaven than to earth; inland plains grassy and flowery, dotted with groves, and extending like seas all around to the rim of the sky; lakes and streams shining and singing, outspread in sheets of mazy embroidery, in untraceable, measureless abundance, brightening every landscape, and keeping the ground fresh and fruitful forever; forests of evergreens growing close together like leaves of grass, girdling a thousand islands and mountains in glorious array; mountains that are monuments of the work of ice; mountains, monuments of volcanic fires; gardens filled with the fairest flowers, giving their fragrance to every wandering wind; and far to the north, thousands of miles of ocean ice, now wrapped in fog, now glowing in sunshine, through nightless days, and again shining in wintry splendor beneath the beams of the aurora—sea, land and sky one mass of white radiance, like a star. Storms, too, are here, as wild and sublime in size and scenery as the landscapes beneath them, displaying the glorious pomp of clouds on the march over mountain and plain, the flight of the snow when all the sky is in bloom, trailing rain-floods, and the booming plunge of avalanches and icebergs and rivers in their rocky glens, while multitudes of wild animals and wild people, clad in feathers and furs, biting, loving, getting a living, make all the wildness wilder.'"

"What exquisite language!" exclaims Miss Elliott.

"And yet," the priest returns, "I find more to admire in an article called 'Life on the Alaska Mission,' which Father Barnum, the Jesuit, published in the *Sacred Heart Messenger* two years before the Klondike became such a universal fad."

"Were the Jesuits really in Alaska, sir, two whole years ago?" question Herbert and Allen with lively interest.

"'Two whole years ago?'" echoes Father Edwards with fine scorn. "Why, Father Pascal Tosi (who died last January—Lord rest him!) and Father Aloysius Robaut went there with Archbishop Seghers to found a mission in *1886!* It was *souls*—not gold—that brought the Jesuits to the Yukon."

"If I remember rightly," says Mrs. Kirke, "Father Barnum drew a picture of Alaska wholly different from that of Mr. Muir. Didn't he write that all that there presents itself to the eye is 'a cold gray sea, with a cold gray stretch of country, covered with a cold gray sky'?"

"Yes, but he admits that what has been written of the grandeur and marvels of Alaska scenery, and all these brilliant accounts (such as Muir's) of its glaciers, its volcanoes, etc., refer to southeastern Alaska, which, in plain talk, is a horse of another color."

"The contrasts must be like those of northern and southern New Zealand, I suppose?" says Miss Margaret.

"What is a *casino*, Father?" puts in Herbert. "Cousin Lex wrote me that we ought to have a *casino* on our Klondike."

"Great Scott! what a silly!" laughs Allen. "Why, Bert, what else should a casino be but an excursion-house, like the big one over at Shell Beach?"

"Beg pardon, Master Allen," says Father Edwards; "Herbert's *casino*, or the *Kashga* of Alaska, is all that, and very much more. It is, as Father Barnum tells us, the exchange, club-house, restaurant, workshop, bath-house, hospital, theatre, as well as hotel, of an Alaska village. It even serves at need for the chapel of the missionary."

"What does it look like?" asks Allen, a good deal taken down.

"Like a cellar with a roof over it. The only light and ventilation are gotten by a little opening at the top, protected by a curtain made of fish-skin. Most of the Alaskan food, according to our good Jesuit, is of the foulest sort. I am almost afraid of destroying your appetite for lunch, ladies," continues the priest, " but really these queer people seem to feast mainly upon rotten salmon and codfish and on bad goose eggs, with a *mayonnaise* of stale seal oil."

" Mercy on us ! doesn't it make them sick ? " cries Margaret.

"Certainly it does; and when it comes to doctoring them, the missionaries have their own time of it. The patients insist on drinking castor-oil like a delicious cordial; and they slowly chew liver-pills, as we might a chocolate caramel. The only drug they dislike is Epsom salts. As a people, they never use any form of salt."

" It must be a dreadful place to live in ! " says Mrs. Kirke with a shudder.

" Dreadful, indeed," agrees the priest. " Think of the cold—in winter fifty and sixty degrees below zero. Then, the long dreary nights, lasting from two in the afternoon until ten the next morning. And the *silence !* They say *that* is terrible. As far as the eye can reach, one unbroken sheet of snow—everything frozen, motionless, soundless, desolate, *dead!*"

"Poor Lex and Lee!" groans Mrs. Kirke. "How can they ever travel to their journey's end through such a living tomb?"

"By dog-sleds, I presume," says Father Edwards. "They say the thoroughbred Arctic dog is a very strong and handsome animal. Father Barnum compares them to half-tamed wolves—yet cowardly, at that. He says they do not bark: but the whole pack will howl in chorus for hours, which must be remarkably cheerful for their owners. Let me read to you," adds the priest, "an abbreviated account of one day's journey (on a dog-sled) given by our good Jesuit: *

"'First we bring the sled inside to load it. It is about nine feet long, and only eighteen inches wide. It rests very low on the ground, and has a cross-bar at the end by which it is guided. The frame-work is laced together with little thongs of sealskin; no nails or screws are used in its construction, hence it is very elastic, and able to withstand the frequent upsets and the many rude

* Messenger of the Sacred Heart, August, 1895.

shocks which it will receive on the way. Before loading up, we will extend this large canvas sheet over the sled and push it well down inside, and let the edges hang over. You will see what it is for in a few moments. Now we are ready for the baggage, and we can carry only what is absolutely necessary. The tea-kettle, frying-pan, a few dishes and the axe, these will do to start with; all the lighter articles are placed in the front part. Next comes a bag of tea, and then a sack of flour; these two things form our main support on the way. We will bring bread enough for a day or two. The next bag holds a little sugar and a few other provisions. Now comes a very important item, a bag of leaf-tobacco, which we will place in such a manner as to get at it easily. This is not for ourselves. It is simply the *currency* of the country and intended for trading with the natives. If we should run out of provisions, we shall have to buy fish for ourselves and the dogs; besides we shall have to hire guides from time to time, so you see the need of the tobacco-bag. Next come our valises and the case with the portable altar; these are heavy, so we place them along the bottom of the sled, towards the rear, and put our rolls of blankets on top of them, which will form a good seat, when we have a chance to use it. This fills the sled, so we fold over the edges of the sheet, tuck it well in and lace a small rope all along the top. This sheet keeps the snow out and holds everything together, so that when upsets occur, nothing can tumble out. The next morning we say Mass very early. Then we dress for the journey.

"'Our *maraartun* [head-runner] is all ready, and so he starts off at a lively gait. One of us is at the end of the sled to steer and keep it steady, and you are comfortably seated on it, for being present in spirit only, you will not freeze.

"'Those who were holding the dogs jump aside, we shout good-by and the team dashes off in grand form. We hope it is a fair start, for we are used to having several false starts, so for a few moments we are in suspense. We have to pass near the edge of the village and there are several *caches* close by our way. These are the little storehouses of the natives, and are always erected on four high posts which afford splendid opportunities for a tangle.

"'We fly by the first one all right, and you remark complacently that the leading dog, "old Cherrywanka," is a fine *chanlista*. At the second cache we are not so lucky. Cherrywanka clears it, but the pair behind him stupidly swerve and take the other side. There is just time to guide the sled by safely, and in an instant we are in a tangle. Some of the dogs have been violently knocked down by the sudden shock, and all of them are snapping viciously at one another, howling, jumping around, and making the tangle as complicated as possible. However, as we were somewhat prepared for this one, we turn the sled over, and get to work among them so quickly that they are soon clear; then we right the sled and off we go again. The object of upsetting the sled is to prevent our unruly team from running away with it before we are ready.

"'We are clear of the village at last and go down the shore over a long slope of hard snow, which leads us out upon the sea. Our maraartun is far ahead of us by this time, as all our delays and tangles are in his favor. The dogs settle down well to work, and as the ice is very smooth we fairly fly along. No team of horses, whether cayuse, broncho, or blue-grass, could keep up with us. However, this is entirely too good to last, and accordingly the sled strikes a piece of ice and is capsized in an instant. It occurred so suddenly that you had no time to jump, and were sent heels over head. These accidents are very frequent. We are far from the shore at present, and so we keep a sharp lookout for cracks in the ice. Wide stretches of open water occur also, and this is one of the great dangers to which a person is exposed when caught on the sea at night or by a storm. Every winter some of our people while out hunting seals are caught on floes and carried off.

"'In the meanwhile, we have been gliding along very nicely, and have come to a wide bay which we have to cross. One glance shows us that there is plenty of trouble at hand for us now. The entire sweep of the bay is very rough—great sheets and jagged blocks of ice are piled up everywhere in wild confusion. The scene resembles a vast marble quarry. Our progress is very slow and tedious. We have to assist the team, push the sled up the steep ice hills, and guide it between the very high blocks. In spite of all our efforts the dogs are constantly entangling themselves around sharp pinnacles of ice, and the sled is constantly upsetting, so altogether, the next three hours are full of trials.

" 'At last, we reach the shore, and stop to take tea at a little village of three or four huts. The dogs are exhausted and immediately curl up in the snow, and we carry what we need into the gloomy casino. Our maraartun kindles a little fire on the floor and fills the kettle with clean ice. We are too cold yet to approach the heat, and when we are able to move about freely, we put some of the frozen bread to thaw, and have tea. Our attendants quickly finish the contents of the kettle, and the precious tea leaves are greedily received by the few residents who have been squatting around staring at us. We then inquire whether there are any sick persons in the settlement, or any infants to be baptized, and, if so, we attend to them; otherwise we replace our things in the sled, straighten out the dogs and start.'"

"Are the missionaries able to do much with these people who cost them such terrific hardships?" asks Miss Elliott, as the priest pauses in his reading.

"The harvest may not seem to us proportionate to the labor and the zeal," returns Father Edwards. "The Jesuits have three or more missions in Alaska, employing about nine Fathers and six Brothers. At the chief mission, the Holy Cross, on the right bank of the Yukon, they have a church, residence, and a boarding-school, where some seventy Indian children are taught by the heroic Sisters of St. Anne.

"Father Barnum gives a funny description of the missionaries' mode of announcing Sundays and holidays to the natives. He says:

"'When a white pennant displaying a red cross is hoisted during the afternoon, they know that on the morrow they must come to Mass.

When the Stars and Stripes float from the mission flagstaff, then they know that it is some American holiday. They watch the flagpole very closely. Once, when the Brother incautiously strung up a brace of wild geese, as the readiest means of placing them in safety, the vigilant observer construed the new signal as an invitation to dine with us, and promptly responded.'"

"I think I should despair of teaching such creatures!" says Miss Elliott, with a dreary sort of laugh.

"And yet," urges the priest, "the missionaries have their consolations, and even their fun —as you have seen. Father Barnum records that 'the children are very bright and learn rapidly. They have been taught the *Tantum Ergo*, and about twenty more Latin hymns. They sing the *Kyrie, Gloria, Credo*, and all the responses of the Mass, with such precision that, were it not for one thing only, want of pocket-handkerchiefs, you might imagine yourself at St. Francis Xavier's, in New York, or even in the Sistine Chapel. We have one young boy in the choir, a half-breed cherub, with a voice like a bird.' He goes on to say," adds Father Edwards, "that 'among our Eskimo there are no names special to each sex, neither are the names permanently retained. They usually signify common objects or natural traits, such as Big Knife—Long Pole—Sore Eyes—Lazy Bones (Shanok), etc., and hence afford no clue to relationship or baptism. We always give the parents a card with their child's name on it, and they generally preserve it carefully. Sometimes a woman will come to the mission and hold up a bundle of fur with the query, "What is my baby's name?" whereupon the baptismal record has to be searched in order to refresh the maternal memory.'"

"Aren't you glad you're not an Eskimo?" says Allen, poking Herbert in the ribs. "Fancy being christened '*Sore Eyes*'!"

"Or answering round the *campus* to such a name as '*Lazy Bones*' or '*Blue Nose*'!" retorts Bert.

"Everybody must have blue noses up there from the cold."

"In that case," laughs Allen, "it must be a common thing to hear mothers calling to their kids: 'Come here, Blue Nose No. 1!' 'Look out there, Blue Nose No. 2!'"

"Here come the fishing-party!" says Miss Elliott as a chorus of laughing voices is heard; and over the rocks climbs into sight pretty Nan, leading her merry company of anglers.

Jack and Phil are lugging between them the big creel of crabs—but not a fish is to be seen.

"We had splendid bites," cries Freddie, with his little nose so shiny and sunburned that it is like a bit of buttered toast. "But confound them! they all got away with our bait!"

"They were the biggest fish I ever saw, too!" adds Phil.

"'The biggest fish *I* ever caught
Was the fish that got away!'"

laughs Herbert, as he and Allen rush off to forage for wood and water.

There is plenty of dry kindling to be picked up near the Yukon, and a good fresh-water spring down among the rocks.

Veva and Jeannie bestir themselves to light

the camp-stove with such wood as is at hand; and Margaret puts on the pot for boiling the crabs. While Mrs. Kirke and Nan are looking over the camp supply of crockery with a view to lunch, there is a loud shout from the younger boys:

"Hello! Aunt Grace and the kids have come!"

And there, sure enough, Captain Saltee has just landed from his sail-boat on the tiny pier, a lady whom Father Edwards advances to greet, and two little lads whom Jack and Fred welcome with uproarious delight.

## VI.

Mrs. Grace Kirke is what Philip calls "an all-round Aunty." She is, indeed, aunt to all our young picnickers, as we will now proceed to show.

She has been twice married. Her first husband, John Winchester, was an uncle of our young friends of that name. Lex and Lee, now in Alaska seeking gold, are the sons of John Winchester, who died when they were little children. Some years after his death, Aunt Grace had married Mr. Herbert Kirke, elder brother to Philip's father, who in his turn, soon left her a widow with twin boys, now nearly six years old.

These little fellows are known as Vaisey and Tasey. Their full names are Gervase and Protase. Having been born and baptized on the feast of Saints Gervase and Protase, Father

Edwards had begged to name them after the twin-martyrs of Milan.

They are very lively little chaps, with not much of the saint about either of them ; and they are more inclined, by their merry pranks, to make martyrs of their friends and relatives than of themselves.

They are as alike as two peas in a pod, and wear sailor suits of navy blue with broad white collars reaching to their waists, and tarpaulin hats over their long, yellow curls.

They are pretty boys, having the Kirke fairness of hair and skin, with the great dark eyes of their mother, who is a small brunette, once a beauty.

Each leads by a string in his right hand a fat poodle that resembles a walking sausage; each carries under his left arm a pet chicken. To get all this live-stock safely off his boat must have cost Captain Saltee some concern. It may be well to know, right here, that Vaisey's poodle is named Cute; and Tasey's, Bute (short for Beauty, and not the Marquis).

It may be of interest also to state that Vaisey's

hen is christened Speckle, and Tasey's Buttercup.

Speckle is a Plymouth Rock—gray, stern and decorous, as becomes one of a family dating back to the landing-place of the Pilgrim Fathers. Buttercup is a yellow Cochin, gay and easy-going—a golden fluff of feathers, good for nothing on earth but to look pretty and devour her own eggs. This she does on the sly, and then trots around trying to look innocent, with the fringes of the yolks hanging to her guilty bill.

"Here's a dog-house and a hen-coop back of the tent, just like Robinson Crusoe!" cries Freddie to the twins.

And then the fun begins.

Having gotten rid of his charges, it does not take five minutes for Vaisey to poke aside the seaweed blanket from the creel of live crabs; and in two more Tasey is roaring around with the great-grandfather of all the crabs hanging to his chubby forefinger.

On the instant, every boy is up with a stick or a stone; and for a short but bitter while, it seems to be an even chance whether Sir Protase or Sir Cancer will make off with the poor little digit.

Father Edwards comes to the rescue, however, and Mrs. Arthur Kirke (as we will now call her to distinguish her from Aunt Grace) hunts up some old linen rags from the camp. But during the bloody battle two of the crabs escape unseen from the basket, and wriggle away into the salt grass.

They will be heard from later, as we shall see, with startling results.

A good quarter of an hour (which chances to be a particularly bad one for Master Tasey!) elapses before Aunt Grace drops breathless into a camp-chair.

All the wounds have been dressed and the crabs safely landed in the boiling pot.

A general peace is proclaimed in order to give the boys a long-promised treat.

This is to hear Aunt Grace read to them all the letters Cousin Lee and Cousin Lex have sent back to home and friends since the beginning of their journey to Alaska.

Our happy picnickers, old and young, gather and group themselves around Aunt Grace's chair.

Settling her gold-rimmed glasses and opening her precious packet, that important little lady begins:

Seattle, Washington State,<br>August 6, 1896.

*Dearest Mother and Folks:*

No doubt you are looking for a letter from us, and I grasp this chance to write. I suppose you got my telegram from here, and know that we are all right after our long journey. But oh! such a time as we have had! We stopped off at St. Paul and saw cousins Nace and Jim; and we bought quite a good deal of our outfits there. The boys were delighted to see us, and Nace trotted us all over town, helping us wonderfully in our selections. He's a fine fellow, and no mistake. The scenery over the Rocky Mountains was simply magnificent; but when we got into the Alkali country, for about three hundred miles we were nearly smothered with dust. We reached here yesterday, and have everything ready to start to-morrow morning at nine o'clock on the steamship *Queen*, for the Klondike, by way of Dyea.

We have been fortunate enough to meet a couple of fine fellows from Chicago, who are also bound for the gold-fields. One of them is a mining engineer, and we have joined forces, and will cross the Pass together and live in the one cabin. Well, you never saw such an excitement in your life as is to be seen here. Nothing is to be heard on every side but Gold—Gold—Gold! It reminds one of the poet Hood's famous lines. Seattle is simply wild, and we had the most exciting time getting passage on the steamship—every berth being engaged a week or more ahead. We would never have been able to go if our Chicago friends had not given us half their cabin.

Gracious! if you could only look out over this town and see the people gone *gold-crazy*, it would amaze you! And yet, quite a number of men are coming back daily from Dyea, because of the hard journey over the Pass.

Dearest, *we* are young and strong, and with God's help we are going to push through to the gold-fields, where, from all accounts, we are *sure* we shall make a fortune. We have bought all our outfits, and the four of us will take through about 3500 pounds of provisions— enough, as we figure, to last us a year. We have bought two horses, one boat, sleds, snow-shoes, etc., etc.; and we start with bright prospects, as I don't think we have overlooked anything. One of our new friends has a camera with him, and at the first chance we will send you photos of our camp and other interesting scenes. Now, my dearest mother, make yourself perfectly easy about us. We are well and strong, and full of hope. Take the best care of yourself and the two darling kids; and if we succeed, be in the very best shape to enjoy our fortune with us. We will try to send you some money in the spring, if we have any luck at all. Kiss Vaisey and Tasey for us six times apiece, and give our love to all the Kirkes and Winchesters. We have said the beads every day since we left, and will try to make up for the loss of Mass on Sundays in the wilderness by saying some extra prayers, as you have always taught us to do. God bless you all! We will write again as soon as we get the chance.

Devotedly your sons,
LEX and LEE.

P.S.—Be sure and take good care of yourself, dearest mother, for all the happiness would be gone for us if we came home rich as kings, to find your precious face missing.

On board the Steamship Queen,<br>Off British Columbia, Aug. 9, 1896.

*Dearest Mom and Folks:*

You can see by this letter-head where we are; and, as we hope to pass a steamer going south, either to-night or to-morrow morning, I concluded to drop you a line, although I haven't very much news to tell you as yet. We left Seattle, as we had planned, on the 7th. We have had a pleasant trip. The scenery up through Puget Sound is very grand. The Sound varies from one to three miles in width, and the giant mountains rise from the water's edge on both sides, running up a couple of thousand feet. We have run about five hundred miles from Seattle; and since leaving Victoria (British Columbia) we haven't seen a house for four hundred miles. You cannot imagine how this adds to the grandeur of these vast and lonely surroundings. I heartily wish you were all with us, and I hope if we can make a good "strike" that we can some day bring you over this part of the trip.

We passed a steamer going south early this morning, and she reported to us that the steamer *City of Mexico* was wrecked last night. She ran upon a sunken rock, and went down in four hundred feet of water. But everybody on board was saved, thank God! It was very foggy, and she got off her track some twenty miles, taking the wrong channel. I don't wonder at her mistake, as the channels and straits are innumerable. We have seen lots of whales. The Sound is full of them.

We took all the Vanderbilt party on board at Victoria. I met one of the family years ago, when I was a boy, in South Carolina, and he remembered me, and had quite a chat with me last evening. He wants me to give him some "points" when we get to the Klondike, as he is interested in "grub-staking" some claims there. I am to have another talk with him before we leave the boat. They are to stay on the steamer and return with her again. It is only a pleasure-trip for *them*. We will land at Skaguay Bay about Thursday afternoon. If possible I will write again from there. And after that I cannot say when you will get a letter from us. Oh, if we could only get one from *you* ! But it is impossible, as just now we are nothing more than tramps—here to-day and gone to-morrow. God bless and keep you all ! Love to the kids and all the cousins. Lee joins me in kindest regards.

Your affectionate son,

LEX.

Juneau, Aug. 11, 1896.

*Dearest Mother and Folks:*

Here we are at Juneau ! Got here last night, and leave this morning at 12 o'clock. We have a hundred miles to go before we land at Dyea; and from there we go over the difficult Pass.

I think, however, from what is told us here, that the dangers and hardships are greatly exaggerated; but of course you cannot tell. They all tell you, though, that there is plenty of gold up there. We have several ladies with their husbands going on into the mines. It is raining here this morning. I have just gotten back to the ship from town. A big thriving place is this Juneau—and queer to Eastern eyes. I wish you could see this mass of dark, mighty mountains, with the wide city lying at its feet, and all its long wharves crowded now with traffic.

I got a large tent for our party of four. We will have altogether about two tons and a half of stuff. They say that the Stewart River is the best place to strike for, as two fellows whom we met last night, and who have just returned from there, took out in seven days one hundred and fifty pounds of gold!

We hope to strike a claim like that. We both wish we could hear from you before we start into the mines; but I am afraid that this will be impossible, as there will not be another vessel up for a week, and we will have left Dyea before that time. We are bracing ourselves for the battle which we have yet to fight, with the hope of our all being together once again in the near future. This may be the last letter which we can send you for some time, but do not worry if you do not hear from us until spring. We are all right now, and propose to keep so.

Yours affectionately,

LEX.

Porcupine Hill in the Mountains,

August 23, 1896.

*Dearest Mother and Folks:*

We are delighted to take the chance of sending you a letter to let you know how we are getting along. We landed at Skaguay Bay, which is about four miles from Dyea Pass, as we find that almost every one is going by this route. The Skaguay Pass is about twelve miles longer, but is not nearly so steep. We have now been about ten days on the trip, and are only about twelve miles in the mountains. You can see by this that our progress is slow. We have about forty-five hundred pounds of stuff, which we have to carry partly with the aid of four donkeys, and partly on our backs. It takes about nine trips to move it all; that is, we move our camp about five miles forward, and then we start and carry all our stuff up to it, and move ahead four or five miles further. At the rate at which we are now getting on I am afraid that we will have to camp all winter at Lake Linderman, as we have about thirty-five miles further to go, and only about from four to six weeks at the latest before winter sets in in earnest. If the lake is frozen up when we reach there we will have to build a log cabin and stay there for the winter; but we are making every effort to get through, and hope, with the help of God, to be able to do so. The trail is almost impassable in places; what with mud, rocks and about five hundred horses, we are detained sometimes for two or three hours. The mountains are several thousand feet in height, and you go up one and down another, as I say, about forty-five miles. They kill on an average some four horses a day, either through packing them too heavily or through some of the beasts sliding over cliffs from weakness and overwork. One horse, ahead of us, fell five hundred feet, and lit in the top of a tree, pack and all. The men got to work, cut the tree down, and started the animal on the trail again, not at all hurt as far as we could judge. There would be no danger of this kind if they would not work their horses so much, but the poor beasts become so weak that when they come to a very narrow place on the Pass they cannot keep their feet, and over they go.

I hope you are all as well as we are, for really the hard work seems to agree with us. Hoping soon to be able to write you the good news that we have gotten through this fall, I am, as ever,

Your own<br>LEE.

We will write you as soon as we have any good news. Be sure and pray for us!

## VII.

Porcupine Hill,
September 8, 1896.

*Dear Folks:*

I have again a chance to write you, which I gladly avail myself of. We are well, thank God! But I will tell you candidly that we need vigorous health, as in our endeavors to reach the gold-fields we are going through the hardest ordeal that either man or beast could experience. All that we have read at home about the difficulties to be encountered on this dreadful Pass you can multiply by three.

The trail lies over mountains thousands of feet high, where you have to jump from rock to rock (and where a misstep means a fall down a precipice five hundred feet deep), and then through mud up to your waist, through rapids and rushing waters. This, and much more, have we gone through since our last letter to you. Many are selling their outfits and going back, appalled by the dangers, etc.; but we are still pushing onwards, moving our two tons of provisions about half a mile a day over these mountains, with the dogged determination of reaching the Alaskan gold-fields or dying in the attempt. There will be very few get in this fall, owing to the expense of having provisions packed over the trail to the lakes, a distance of forty-five miles. You will get some faint idea of the cost when I tell you that they offered to land our provisions these forty-five miles for one dollar per pound, or a matter of *four thousand dollars!* We are now advanced on the trail about fifteen miles, and we have still about thirty to go, which we think will take us until the winter sets in. We are writing this in our tent, on the top of a range of mountains at least twelve hundred feet high. On the right is a rushing torrent dashing over the rocks in boiling cascades. On the left is a deep ravine. The trail passes twenty feet in front of our tent. Do we sleep well? Well, I should say so! After plugging up and down the mountain, packing, we turn in about eight or nine o'clock, and up again at four A.M., on the push. I tell you it is labor, and no mistake.

You would not know your two dudes, dear mother, if you were to meet them face to face. I have not seen my countenance for weeks. All on the trail look very much the same, viz., like a set of tramps; and we meet here on our travels all kinds and conditions of men. Well, good-by, until we get the chance to write again.

LEX.

Aunt Grace lays aside her glasses, wipes her eyes, which the sight of her dear exiles' letters always dims, and looking around her, asks:

"Will somebody run over to the cove and see if the tide is up? I don't want the little ones to lose their bath."

Two or three somebodys rush off to a little smooth horse-shoe of sand which affords a nice bathing-place among the rocks. There is a good-sized bath-house there as well.

Jack is the first one back.

"High tide!" he announces out of breath, for Phil and Fred have almost outrun him in the race. "And I tell you, that sun's as hot as a mustard-plaster!"

"Come, boys," cries Father Edwards, "let's all go and take a bath. Make your mind easy, Mrs. Kirke, I'll see to the twins. Come, Vaisey—come Tasey!"

And away they go trooping, the priest and the seven boys, with the dogs at their heels.

"What a comfort Father Edwards is!" sighs Mrs. Grace; "nothing is a trouble to him. It is perfect rest to know the children are safe in his care."

Meanwhile the girls have moved the camp-chairs to the other side of the tent to escape the sun, which (as Jack has declared) is now, indeed, "as hot as a mustard-plaster."

All settle themselves comfortably. Aunt Grace and her sister-in-law take out certain bits of lace-work they have brought in their bags. Nan nestles at her mother's feet, and leans her pretty head against her knee.

"Momsie dear," she says, "I'm all tuckered

out. That fishing excursion, without any fish, has worn me threadbare. I don't wonder *Josiah Allen's Wife* calls it an '*exertion*.'"

"Certainly it is an 'exertion,'" assents Mrs. Kirke smiling. "By the way, I've always thought *Josiah Allen's Wife* said a particularly good and true thing when she advised all picnickers on the return trip from an 'exertion' not to talk."

"Why?" ask the girls.

"Because, as she says, every one after a long day's outing is apt to be tired and nervous, and consequently cross and unreasonable. Pie and pickles sometimes work sad havoc with one's temper—to say nothing of cake and lemonade."

Veva and Jeannie by this time have brought out the camp-table from the tent, and Miss Elliott, with Olive's help, begins to spread the lunch.

It is high noon, and the bathers will not be back for an hour. The chickens have been feeding on some tid-bits the girls have flung them.

"Come here, Buttercup, and be nursed," calls

Nan. "You'll get the dyspepsia if you eat any more."

The tame creature obeys at once, and cuddles down in Nan's lap like a pet cat. She has such a wealth of golden feathers that she fills the girl's lap, and she literally purrs under the caressing strokes of the pretty white hand.

"Come here, Speckle," laughs Olive, "you shall not be neglected. You poor old Plymouth Rock! come over here, and tell me all about the Pilgrim Fathers and the Pilgrim Mothers!"

"And their sisters and their cousins and their aunts," adds Nan, as Speckle leaps up to Olive's knee, and looks rather shamefaced under the unusual caresses.

"Girls, you'll spoil those hens," suggests Veva, arranging the cups and saucers. While Jeannie calls to Miss Elliott: "Cousin Margaret you've dropped your bag. Isn't that a letter that has fallen out of it?"

Margaret sinks into a chair, and begins to laugh.

"Was there ever such a stupid?" she cries, picking up the bag and turning out its contents.

"Of course it is a letter; and here is a package besides. The post-boy gave them to me this morning just as I boarded the car at the Inlet. I stuffed them into my bag and forgot all about them. Now, with your permission, ladies, I'll look at the letter, which I think is from my dear old Sister Alacoque at St. Xavier's."

Presently she lifts her smiling eyes to Jeannie, with the question:

"Do you remember my speaking of Gertrude de Venne—the beautiful French girl who was at St. Xavier's for a time?"

"Yes; is she married?" asks her cousin.

"Joined the Carmelites," returns Miss Elliott. "Sister Alacoque has often promised to tell me a story about Gertrude's mother and another remarkable girl, who were the leading spirits in the old convent-school in France, where Sister was educated. This"—and she raises a roll of thin foreign paper from her lap, "this is the story at last."

"Oh, *please* read it to us!" plead Veva and Jeannie.

"It seems to be very childlike," says Margaret, turning the leaves and skimming through them. "My good old Sister of Mercy writes quite simply—a plain unvarnished tale. Maybe it will prove too tame for your tastes—'milk for babes!'—eh, Nan?"

"So much the better!" says Mrs. Kirke. "There are no critics here; and it is far too hot for 'strong meats' to-day. I, for one, am sick of the heavy, sensational stories of the period."

"And I;" murmurs Aunt Grace. "One tires of the lurid realism of even Sienkiewicz and Corelli."

"Well, here goes!" cries Miss Elliott, straightening out her roll of paper. "If it bores you, it is easy to tell me to stop. Sister calls her story

### AN EXAMPLE IN ALGEBRA.

It did not seem a hard example, but she could not do it. She had worked at it several hours each day for the week past. She had pored over it for the entire afternoon. At six o'clock she was to go to class. And without it? So it seemed.

After a moment's thinking, she arose from

her little table, and stood by the window. One long glance at the beautiful country landscape in the November twilight; and then she spoke to herself aloud and reprovingly:

"Nothing has ever conquered you yet, Gertrude—nothing! There never was a lesson—a duty, which you did not face and vanquish. And now, at the age of eighteen, an algebra example? Shame!"

She walked up and down her little room, her brows contracted, her hands clasped behind her.

"My father died at the cannon's mouth, committing his soul to God. My mother—so the nuns tell me—bore years of suffering like a heroine, and died like a saint. If heredity has any power at all, I ought to be a marvel; yet here I am, foiled by a simple example in algebra! The fact is humiliating."

## VIII.

A GENTLE knock at the door was followed by the entrance of a fair and lovely girl of about Gertrude's age.

"How fierce you look!" she exclaimed, laughing lightly.

"And fierce I feel," returned Gertrude, without discontinuing her walk. "Do you know, Aimée, I cannot solve that last example in algebra?"

"Is that all, Gertrude? I feel relieved! I feared something of moment." And Aimée joined her friend in her walk.

"I do not like to fail in anything. I never have failed before. I do not know from personal experience what failure means."

"Ah, Gertrude," said her friend sweetly, "do you remember what Mother St. Louis told you when she was dying—that she would procure some great favor for you on the feast of St. Gertrude, if on that day she was in heaven?"

"Of course I remember it! And to-morrow will be St. Gertrude's feast. It is her feast already, isn't it? The feasts of the blessed begin, they say, on their vigils."

"Her feast already, dear, and perhaps—" Aimée hesitated.

Gertrude looked impatient.

"Perhaps what?" she inquired.

"Perhaps the favor lies in your *not* getting that example, Gertrude."

"You say that, Aimée? And do you realize all the getting of that example may mean to me? Do you forget that Professor Ribaut has promised to assist me in getting into the School of Technology over in America, or into the University at Glasgow, or into the National School of Science here in France—or, at least, to get for me the direction of the teachers at one of these places? Of course I prefer America, my parents' country and mine—"

Aimée was silent for a moment or two before

answering; then she laid her hand on Gertrude's arm, and said in a solemn tone:

"Gertrude, I have been thinking how much the not getting of the example may mean to you. I will say no more now. You wish, it would seem, not to understand me. But I will pray for you, Gertrude, that you may understand me before long. You are my dearest friend."

It was now Gertrude's turn to be silent, but as they stood together by the window, she beat the floor nervously with her foot.

"I wish not to fail in my lesson. I never fail in anything. What has my whole record been here at school for the past ten years but one of vigorous efforts—and successes?"

"There are lessons in life, Gertrude, which are worth more than book-learning to us; science fades before them. They are the lessons in which God Himself instructs the heart."

"You are very wise, Aimée," said her friend, with that intense respect which virtue always excites in the truly noble, "and very sweet in your wisdom. There is the bell for recitation! Let us go. Sister likes to have us in class before she comes."

As Professor Ribaut greeted his pupils in the large hall, his expression of welcome merged into one of keen admiration as Gertrude McDonald passed before his desk.

"Miss McDonald," he inquired, as soon as the class were seated, "have you solved that problem in algebra? And are you ready to demonstrate the last proposition in geometry?"

The color rose to Gertrude's cheeks as she replied:

"I have demonstrated the proposition, Professor, but the problem I have not yet solved."

A shadow passed over the master's face.

"I am disappointed! Not one member of the faculty in Paris could work out that problem. I told them I had a pupil—a young lady—who would not fail to get it. They have promised me to petition the opening of the School of Science to women, if I can bring them the problem solved by one. *I am disappointed!*"

## IX.

His tone was so bitter that a thrill ran through the youthful assembly—a thrill of keen and sympathetic disappointment. Every eye turned to Gertrude. She had been the intellectual idol of her class; but it seemed to them all (even as to her own heart) at this trying moment, that the idol had fallen. They had regarded her as a genius. Like herself, they had held the opinion that failure in anything was not for her. It had been at her urgent desire that Mother St. Francis had allowed the professor to direct a class in advanced mathematics at the convent. It was she who had inspired thirty other girls with the same ambition and industry that directed her own studies. Professor Ribaut had never looked to her intelligence in vain. Now, when he looked to it and leaned upon it with the most eager anxiety —with a vivid sense that his own reputation as a teacher was at stake—he was doomed to painful disappointment.

Gertrude's voice was always very sweet and clear, but now it seemed to assume an added softness in tone, as she ventured to say:

"One may be able to do in two weeks what has not been accomplished in one. I will try the problem again, professor. Or, it may be, some other member of the class has the correct result."

The other pupils smiled, half in amusement, half in denial.

The rest of the work was taken up by the class, but there was little spirit manifested. The usual strict attention seemed gone. The work was all difficult, and it had been well prepared, but the attendant Sister, who sat writing at her desk in one corner of the room, remarked the dulness of the recitation, as she had also remarked its cause. When the hour had expired Professor Ribaut bade his pupils a courteous good evening. He paused a moment before passing out of the door.

"Miss McDonald, I will not give up hope," he said; "I will wait another week."

Gertrude smiled her gratitude, and then went over to Sister's desk.

"You saw my humiliation, Sister," she said quietly.

"Yes," said the Sister, with tender sympathy in her voice.

"I am never to get that example. Sister, I feel I am not. However, I will try."

All the pupils had now left the hall.

Sister and Gertrude remained a while speaking together, and then Gertrude went to the chapel.

She had always prayed a great deal over her lessons; she had always claimed that in the chapel she had obtained through earnest petition all that had made her the admiration of the school. She had always said: "If one is not living and working for God alone, what is she in this world for? She ought to seek another."

Everything had seemed vain to her which was not directed in some way to Him who from earliest infancy she had been taught to reverence, serve and love.

Now she knelt in the chapel alone.

She felt sure that the feast of St. Gertrude was already being celebrated in heaven, that even then the great and powerful saint was dispensing favors to her clients and to those recommended to her intercession. Gertrude bowed her head and prayed as she had never prayed before—as only the humble soul knows how to pray—feeling that the Sacred Heart was near with a newness of love, and regarding the mediation of the saints as one of the dearest of graces.

The week passed away. Gertrude had worked at the problem; but when the evening for recitation came, it was to see her still with no satisfactory result to present to Professor Ribaut. What her interior combat had been, perhaps no one—not even Mother St. Francis or dear Aimée—ever suspected.

Time passed on. The example seemed forgotten, but all that followed from it was peculiarly emphatic. Every one's manner seemed changed. Gertrude had never been a very talkative girl, but now she grew strangely silent —not with a proud and sullen silence, but with a most thoughtful and prayerful reserve.

## X.

A YEAR went by.

It was again the 14th of November, the vigil of St. Gertrude's feast.

Mother St. Francis sought Gertrude's room.

"I have a letter from your cousin in Boston, your guardian, Gertrude," she said, as Gertrude rose from her chair to welcome her, "and he informs me that a gentleman in connection with the United States Navy, who at present resides in Boston, is willing to take you as his pupil. He was formerly a professor at a scientific school in New York, and your cousin says he is one of the leading men of our day in civil engineering and all kindred subjects."

Gertrude listened respectfully until Mother St. Francis had finished speaking. Then she looked at the floor and out of the window before replying. At length she inquired: "What does my cousin wish me to do?"

"He leaves the decision entirely to me," returned the nun, "and I feel that, though the sacrifice is one both for our school and for myself personally, I ought to let you go. Your cousin and his wife, whom I have long known, are model Catholics. You will reside with them. Your one aspiration for years has been to become a teacher, and this opportunity for improvement is so excellent a one, it does not seem right in me to keep you from it. You are now nineteen years old—a fact that greatly influences my decision. I have already prayed over the matter, but it seemed clear to me from the first that I ought to let you go."

The tears were in Gertrude's eyes. She drew a second chair near the window and they sat down together.

"Mother," said Gertrude gravely, "my mind has been steadily changing since the vigil of the feast of my patron saint, a year ago to-day. Then I did long to be a teacher—a professor—thoroughly prepared for an able and long career. I see now how vain were my best hopes. I see what possibilities of failure—perhaps frequent failure—would await me. The very possibility itself would gnaw all the peace and happiness out of my life. I have been thinking that for a character like mine there ought to be a profession where failures are impossible. Where I begin, where I labor, I must succeed."

Mother St. Francis laid her hand gently over Gertrude's.

"My dear child, failures are sometimes best for us all. God does not look to the result, but to the effort."

"That is exactly what I mean, Mother. I must have some work in life, some career, where only *effort* is considered. Then there could be nothing but a series of successes."

Mother St. Francis sighed. She saw clearly that God Himself was dealing with the heart of this dear child.

"Where did you get all these ideas, Gertrude? When did you begin to have this view of life and of your life-work?"

"When I failed to get that algebra example

last year. Mother, I wouldn't wish to get it now. I would rather save my soul first."

Gertrude's look and tone added a strange, deep meaning to her words.

The Mother smiled, but she respected the sincerity with which Gertrude spoke.

"To-morrow, dear," she said, rising, "will be the feast of St. Gertrude. We will pray, we will implore her intercession at our communion, that you may be guided only by God's holy will."

As Mother St. Francis bade Gertrude goodnight, Aimée entered the room, and for an hour the two friends conversed together much more seriously and religiously than they had ever conversed before.

It was decided the next day, even by Gertrude herself, that she had better return to America; and before Christmas she was installed at her home in Boston, and had begun her lessons with her new instructor. Her cousins were extremely proud of her. Dignified and reserved of manner, yet sweet and courteous in her intercourse with others, she seemed a person whose great influence in the world might be easily prophesied. The hearts of her family found in her their delight; and the sorrow, disappointment and humiliation of the other side of the sea might have been forgotten. So it probably would have been by many another, but for Gertrude, even in the midst of her brilliant work, in the midst of sweet domestic happiness and the constant admiration of a host of friends, there ever loomed before her mental gaze the one failure of her life—*an unsolved example in algebra.*

\* \* \* \*

Forty years have passed away; and only a month ago there entered at the Carmelite Convent in a well-known city of America a young French girl named Gertrude de Venne. She was greeted by the Superior, a venerable religious of sixty years, whose infirmities, cares, constant fasts and long vigils rendered her feeble and aged long before her time, but in her glance and smile there were a sweetness and a freshness which increasing years, through increasing holiness, would make only more and more heavenly. Her name was Mother Gertrude of the Heart of Jesus, and the dear girl to whom she was giving her holy welcome was the youngest child and only daughter of her old school friend, now Madame Aimée de Venne.

As the new aspirant to religious life removed her worldly dress she took from her pocket-book a worn yellow paper with faded writing upon it.

"Mamma told me to show you this, dear Mother. She wishes you to know that it has helped her to give me up willingly to God's service. She wishes me to tell you, too, that old Professor Ribaut, whose son now occupies his place in Paris, is still living. He is eighty-seven years old."

Mother Gertrude opened the paper, and the tears rushed to her eyes. Raising her glance to heaven, she sat for a moment wrapped in prayer. The holy calm which ever encompassed her seemed to break away for the time in a rapturous thanksgiving of the heart.

Her little namesake waited a brief space and then murmured:

"Mamma says that example has never yet

been worked out, though even now the younger Professor Ribaut gives it to his pupils. Old heads have declared it cannot be solved."

A week later, when a little trunk of treasures went back to Aimée from the convent which had received her precious child, she found within it a note from her holy old friend.

"My loved Aimée" (it read): "Please give the enclosed solution to Professor Ribaut when you have the opportunity of seeing him, and tell him for me that only to-day the way to procure the correct result came unsought into my mind. It will certainly be a gratification to his professional heart to see the problem solved. Please assure him of my constant grateful remembrance of him before God, and say that now that I am at least in the way of saving my soul through God's mercy, I have little fear in sending him what would have been fatal to me nearly half a century ago—*the correct answer to a most difficult example in algebra.*"

## XI.

As Miss Elliott finishes the old Sister's story, and the girls sit pondering dreamily upon its moral, a chorus of boyish voices is heard singing close at hand:

> "Golden bright as the best champagne,
>   This fair, life-giving sea!
> The old Greeks' cure for a heart in pain
>   Was a bath in its waters free.
> Dreamed they then of this strand of strands,
>   Whose breath one's being thrills?
> An ocean bath on *Klondike* sands
>   Hath cure for all our ills!
>     Yo ho, my lads, yo ho!"

Father Edwards and the boys are back from their bath in a fine glow of spirits. The very poodles seem to have a fresh curl in their saucy tails, and the twins are rosy as little Cupids.

"We are as hungry as wolves!" announces Philip. "Nothing like a bath for giving a fellow an appetite!"

"To give *you* more appetite than you already have," says Nan, "is like carrying coals to Newcastle!"

"Lunch is ready!" proclaims Allen, who has arrayed himself in a white apron of Mrs. Arthur Kirke, and now bows to the assembled company with the grace of a high-class waiter.

"*Le couvert est mis!*" cries Herbert. "Why don't you do it in French, Al?"

"Or in Irish," suggests Jack.

"Don't you know, Jack," says Father Edwards, "that the waiters at all the best hotels in Dublin talk French like Parisians? But, good gracious, boys" (giving a slap at his face as he sits down to lunch), "the mosquitoes are here by the thousands! They'll devour us before we get to the dessert."

"We're supposed to be *in the desert* already, Father," retorts Herbert with a comical smile; "in the desert of the Klondike. *That* swarms with mosquitoes, they say."

"Haven't you a net, young gentlemen?" asks Margaret.

For reply several of the boys rush to the tent

and drag out an enormous roll of red netting. And then the ladies begin to understand the use of four high poles that are sunk in the sand as if to form a large quadrangle, with the camp-table for its centre. They are made from the old masts of a shipwrecked vessel, and the elder boys, who are all experts at hurdling and high-jump, soon show their dexterity by casting the netting over the poles.

The mosquitoes driven out by many hands armed with towels, the airy curtains are dropped to the sand, and our friends, old and young, find themselves in a delightful fairy bower which would throw any civilized dining-room into the shade.

Father Edwards takes up a sandwich and begins to laugh, saying:

"This reminds me of Stockton's funny story, *The Casting Away of Mrs. Lecks and Mrs. Aleshine.* Do you remember, Mrs. Kirke, the account of the comforts and luxuries enjoyed by those worthy women after they were shipwrecked in mid-ocean?"

"Yes," replies Mrs. Arthur Kirke, dispensing

the good things among the party with a liberal hand, "one of the women, I remember, while floating on the water on a life-preserver, actually produces a Bologna sausage and a clasp-knife from her pocket and proceeds to cut slices for her own and her companion's enjoyment."

"And when they finally reach the desert island in safety," recalls Miss Elliott, "they find there a cottage filled with every convenience for their use. Not a creature to be seen in the house, but even white lawn wrappers trimmed with blue ribbons are hanging up in the closets!"

"It seems the very height of the ridiculous," says the priest; "and still, a friend who has travelled in Norway tells me that there in the snow mountains are often to be found little tenantless cabins equipped with beds, coverlets, etc., and rich in cupboards well supplied with lots of canned goods."

"For the use of the mountain-fairies?" asks Mrs. Grace Kirke smiling.

"No; for the use of tourists. My friend says that the spirit of that land is so honest and trusting that the owner of the cabins allows all travellers to help themselves to the beds and food, according to their needs, with the understanding (which is universal) that each shall deposit on the window-sill inside the cottage, just as *Mrs. Lecks* and *Mrs. Aleshine* did in the jars on the mantel-shelf, as much money as he or she considers a just compensation."

"But don't the tramps steal the money?" says Miss Elliott.

"It seems not," replies the priest. "The owner of these mountain cabins stocks them with food in April, and then goes his way. He does not return to them until October, when he collects his dues from unknown and long-gone boarders—finding the window-sill piled thick with coins."

"Such a plan of collecting board-money would not work well in America," says Aunt Grace, as she gives an apple-tart to each of the twins, and flings some cheese to the poodles.

Then the talk trails off into a sober chat among the elders of the party on questions of foreign and domestic morality.

This does not interest the younger fry. The

girls, enjoying their cakes and tea, begin to discuss in an undertone the story of Gertrude McDonald; while the boys draw close together and between huge mouthfuls of pie exchange views on foot-ball and base-ball, detailing the names of fellows they know on the newest "teams."

Their voices rise by degrees, until such terms as "left field," "centre field," "first base," "second base," "short-stop," "pitcher and catcher," are heard above all the rest of the talk.

When every one else has paused to listen, Phil is heard in a solitary roar:

"You bet, when Dick Hare was short-stop and tried to stop that big inshoot with his head—there was something wrong with the mask, and the ball broke every bone in his face!"

"Horrible!" cries Father Edwards. "That's what I call brutal play! 'Broke all the bones in his face,' did you say? How many bones are there in the human face, Phil?"

"Don't know, sir," replies Kirke rather abashed.

"Fourteen, sir," says Herbert, who is well up in his anatomy, with dreams of being a doctor some day.

"Correct," assents the priest, adding: "My brother is house-surgeon in a New York hospital, and he tells a queer story about a man there who had broken all the bones of his face. Not with base-ball or foot-ball, either. He was an Irishman named Jimmy Hogan, and he worked in a five-story elevator on the wharf. One day he was standing just within the door on the second floor when he heard a voice cry: 'Look out there!' Jimmy thought it was really an invitation for him to look out and up, which he did; and on the instant an iron weight of fifty pounds fell full on his face!"

"Ugh!" shudder all the ladies, while some of the boys give long, low whistles of sympathetic surprise.

"Fact," says Father Edwards. "When they fetched him to the hospital the doctors set about repairing the damages. He was a horrible sight, brother says—his face a mass of bloody jelly. The queer part of it was that none of them had ever seen the man before the accident. They had nothing to guide them in building up his face again. 'Let's make him as handsome as we can!' said one of the surgeons. So they patched and mended as well as science helped them to do—made him a Roman nose, and straightened out all the dents; filled in with oakum, and rounded off all the ragged edges. Their work was a success. Jimmy came out from under their hands a wonder of manly beauty. Some days after his wounds had healed, his wife came hunting for him. She had been round all the hospitals in New York before she found him. That day, Doc says, they had taken off the bandages, and Jimmy sat beside his cot, dressed, and as handsome and imposing as a Roman senator.* Mrs. Hogan looked him over, and then began to wail: 'That's not my man at all, at all! Sure Jimmy niver looked like *that!*' 'Have you a picture of your husband?' says Doc. ''Deed an' I have!' cries Mrs. Hogan, 'and a good photy of him it is—taken a week before he got hurted.'

* A fact.

'Bring it to-morrow,' says Doc, sending her off—although the Roman senator could be heard declaring the woman to be his true and lawful wife. She came the next day, bringing a photograph of a man who was as ugly as sin, with a pug nose, a retreating forehead, and a wide, smirking mouth. It took some time to convince Mrs. Hogan that she really owned the other (?) handsome man with the Roman nose; but Jimmy and the surgeon, between them, made everything right; and in due time she lugged off her beauty of a boy, as happy (Doc says) as if she had drawn a first prize in a lottery."

This story amuses all, but tickles Philip Kirke more than the others. He laughs, and laughs again, over his dish of boiled crabs, to which he has been devoting himself so industriously that he now sits before a ruin of empty scarlet shells and jagged legs.

"Philip!" cries his mother, "I believe you have eaten up half the crabs. As a penance, you must give us your recitation on 'Crabbing at Shell Beach.'"

"All right!" swaggers Phil, showing great

good-humor. "If you can stand it, I can!" and with a broad grin on his comical, cross-eyed face, he lumbers to his feet, and begins in rather a sing-song fashion:

> "The tide runs low, the salt winds blow
>   Over the briny bay,
> The old drawbridge is a bonny place
>   On a sweet September day.

> "The dull blue waters wash the wharves,
>   The seaweed twines the piers,
> Like the long green hair of a mermaid fair,
>   Wet with her salt, salt tears.

> "*Swish!* goes the line in the dimpling tide—
>   Like rubies the red bait gleams!
> Out of his weedy lair the crab
>   Floats from his noontide dreams.

> "Bewitching *Cancer!* fair to see
>   Are the olive tints of thy shell:
> Thy strong blue claws, thy serrate jaws,
>   Thy jewel'd eyes as well!

> "Full of coquettish grace, approach
>   The bait of the dangling line—
> Quick with the net! Ah, charming pet,
>   Thou'rt safe in this snare of mine!

> "Now to the basket's depths descend
>   And sleep in its gloom profound:
> The while 'neath the lid, securely hid,
>   Cool seaweeds wrap thee round.

> "The sport goes on; the white-wing'd yachts
>   Skim over the glittering bay;
> And now and then to the lock drifts in
>   A sail-boat, sunny and gay.

"The 'fiddlers' wriggle and writhe, and crawl
   To their holes in the dusky loam ;
The pungent, brassy winds of the marsh
   Over the waters come.

"Dance on, grave crabs, in your minuet,
   While the 'fiddlers' gayly play !
Oh, the old drawbridge is a bonny place
   On a sweet September day !"

"Now, Bert, it's your turn," cries Nan. "I don't think Father Edwards has ever heard you recite the lines Cousin Lex wrote to tease Jeannie before he went to Alaska."

"Oh, yes, Bert !" coax all the girls, "give us the 'Eldest Daughter' ! "

And amid much poking and pushing from Phil, Allen and Jack, Herbert finds himself confusedly on his feet, reciting what he calls in his mind, with some contempt, "girl-poetry":

" 'Tis sweet to be the eldest child,
   The first pure pledge of wedded love,
The first dear angel undefiled,
   All other firstlings far above;
But certain 'tis we envy not
The eldest daughter's sorry lot.
'Tis: 'Jeannie, watch the children yonder!
Don't let the boys or baby wander
Among the rocks or near the water!'
'Tis: 'Jeannie, wait!' or: 'Jeannie, hurry!'
Ah, me, how full of care and worry
Is mother's eldest daughter!

"If Freddie stumbles in the pond
   Or Jackie loses hat or shoe,
If Allen's book is illy conn'd
   Or Olive vexes baby Lou,
The eldest sister's patient soul
Must bear the burden of the whole.
'Tis : ' Jeannie, what *has* come to Freddie ? '
' Has Jackie lost that shoe already ? '
' Why wasn't Allen's lesson shorter ? '
' Here, sit by Olive's side, and maybe
' You'll keep the minx from teasing Baby ! '
——Alas ! poor eldest daughter !

" Where selfless tasks must brave be done,
   (Nursing by day or watch by night),
Whene'er, from rise to set of sun,
   A thousand wrongs must be set right,
Beside her mother, grave of face,
The eldest daughter finds her place.
'Tis : ' Jeannie, Jack's a bruise distressing ! '
Or : ' Jeannie, Freddie's cut needs dressing ! '
' Quick ! spread the poultice ! heat the water ! '
——And so it goes—noon, night, and morning,
Reproving, aiding, coaxing, warning.
Heaven help the eldest daughter ! "

"Come on, eldest daughter !" cries Nan springing up, "and all the younger daughters, too. There's plenty of work for idle hands. We've got all these dishes to wash and things to put to rights before Aunt Grace can go on with the boys' letters !"

## XII.

FATHER EDWARDS has finished his office in a little quiet spot over beside the Yukon; and when he comes back, smoking his cigar, he finds the lunch all cleared away, and the entire party sitting under the mosquito-netting waiting his return.

The ladies have taken out their lace-work again, and the girls cluster round Aunt Grace, who is opening her precious packet of letters. She only waits for the priest to be seated to explain that the next Alaskan letter is from Lex to her nephew, Sam Bradleigh.

A wild bird sings its short, sweet broken song in a tree close by; the broad ocean glitters like a mass of diamonds, and a gentle breeze flutters the rose-colored netting, as she begins:

Skaguay Trail, Alaska,
Hotel de Cabin, Sept. 20, 1896.

*My Dear Sam:*

I enclose a letter to each of your boys, in answer to those which they wrote to me. It was a joy to get them. I was greatly pleased to see that they had not forgotten me. We have taken a contract for a man from Skaguay, to build a cabin for him. We have it nearly completed. It puts in the time for us, and keeps us fellows outside where we can get hardened up against the date when we have to be again on the march. We will very often have to sleep right on the snow inside of our sleeping-bags: as it will not pay when we get on the move to pitch a tent for one night's stand. We will just have a big camp-fire built, and we will lie alongside of it. There will be six in our immediate party—that is, travelling companions, but we are three different parties as regards partnership. If we find it is required we will each stand a watch at night and keep up the fire. It is very cold here now; the mercury registers fifteen to twenty-five below.

If you could hear the wind howling through this canyon at night you would think the lower regions had broken loose. They say they have struck it rich at Lake Tagish, about thirty miles from here, but we have been unable to learn if it is true, owing to our having so much difficulty in getting over there. I do not know whether to believe it or not, as there are so many reports going. I saw a man yesterday who came out from Dawson City, and I questioned him closely in regard to the finds. He tells me they are not at all exaggerated. They have started to build a wagon road from Skaguay to Lake Bennett, which I think will eventually be turned into a railroad. They are making a sleigh road, also, up the river; but the snow has not gotten packed down well enough yet for it to be of any use. The Canadian police have about one hundred and fifty dogs at Skaguay waiting until the river trail is fit to pack on. It is surprising to see what loads these dogs will take along. I saw a fellow moving the other day from his tent where he tried to winter (but he could not stand it). He built himself a cabin about half a mile above. He had four dogs, with four hundred pounds on his sleigh, and was going up quite a grade at that. Of course, though, he had a fairish beaten road just at this point.

Tell Mrs. B. I think she would enjoy looking at some of the work done by the Indian women. They display wonderful taste and ingenuity in making fancy articles. If I ever get rich and can afford it, I intend to bring a collection of them home with me.

Their villages are the queerest places you ever saw. They have great quantities of "*totems*," like our American Indians; and these emblems of the tribes are indicated by poles, bearing idols which they worship in some sort of fashion. Some of these idols are twenty feet high, with frogs, serpents, men, all carved, one above the other, and painted in the gayest colors. One in particular struck me as being very funny. It was the highest figure on a pole in the village. It represented a man with an immense head, little body and very short legs, surmounted with a large high hat painted green.

The natives have no idea of the value of

money. If they see a thing they fancy, the cost of it has nothing to do with it if they want it. I saw one old fellow give thirty dollars for an old American flag that was worth not more than a couple of dollars. They always ask " How much ? " When you tell them the price they say: " I take him." If you wish to buy from them, and they tell you the price, they would not take off one penny to make a sale.

Write when you can.

With kindest regards, etc.,

I am your friend,

LEX.

Out among the Bears, Alaska,

September 15, 1897.

*My Dear little Freddie:*

I have your interesting little letter before me while I write by the light of one candle in our small cabin; and I tell you one candle, Freddie, doesn't give you much light. But if it takes three hundred and sixty-five candles to do you a year, and if you burn more than one a night, how much weight would you have to carry ? There is an Irishman's sum for you ! Ask your papa if you can do it by algebra or by the rule of thumb ? That is something like the riddle I heard the other day, viz.: " Bean soup is the answer; what is the question ? "

We have seen several bears, but have been unable to get close enough to get a shot at them; and that reminds me of a little incident that happened here lately. There was a bear that came down every night to make his supper on one of the dead horses in the trail, and four brave fellows camped close by thought they would like to kill him. So they built a platform up in a clump of trees near the dead horse during the day, and went back to their cabin and played a game of cards to see who would get the bear's skin after they had killed Bruin. They went to the platform about dark, and waited, armed with rifles. They almost quarrelled as to who should have the first shot at the beast when he came for his supper. Presently Mr. Bear put in an appearance, sniffed around the horse awhile, and then spied the fellows up the tree. He shuffled over till he got under the platform, when he gave an awful growl. "You shoot first!" whispered one. "No, *you* do it," urged another. "Plant your shot right between his eyes!" said a third; when lo! the brute gave another growl, louder and more wicked than the first, and *looked up*, clasping the trunk of the tree with his hairy arms. They all dropped their rifles and fell on their knees on the platform, beginning to pray with all their might. The bear went back to the horse, and they—well, they have never said *bear* since that day.

We killed a couple of mountain-goats last week which made quite a change in our bill of fare. The weather, Fred, is pretty cold here, as the mercury ranges from fifteen to twenty-five below zero, and ice is six feet thick on the river.

If we had you out here I would give you a good ride on a dog-sled. You ought to see them go—four dogs to a sled. I hope you will get your foot-ball team in good shape and give those fellows that beat you before, a good dressing down. I am very sorry about the letters that went to Dawson City, but perhaps they will arrive here before we start. Don't forget to write again when you get the chance.

Your sincere<br>
Lex.

Camp Emergency, Skaguay,<br>
September 21, 1896.

*Dear little Cousin Nan:*

Your jolly little letter was received with your mamma's, and I could imagine I was talking with you by keeping my eye on the pen-sketch of yourself you attached to it. It was so *striking!* I am glad to hear of your art-studies, and of Veva's music and language lessons. I am afraid, as you say in your letter, that after our rough life out here we will be kind of afraid of our two stately and cultivated cousins when we get back to civilized life again. You will want to keep us in the back yard and feed us out of a trough. But look sharp if you do; for we will certainly *bite!*

I wish you could have seen the donkeys, or *burros* (as they call them here), we had when we first started on the trail. They were the cutest things you ever saw. One in particular wasn't much larger than a big St. Bernard dog. He was a funny little fellow. You couldn't keep him tied, and he would follow you all around like a dog; come walking into the tent, pick up one of your boots and start to chew it: then try to get at things on the stove. These donkeys will eat anything, from oats to a tin can. They are like goats in that.

A funny thing happened one night with my little pet while we were on the trail. I was sound asleep in the middle of the night, but woke up suddenly to see something big and dark at the opening of the tent. Supposing it was the donkey, I yelled: "Get out of there, you son of an Alaska *burro!*" when brother Lee shouted from the tent-door: "What's the matter, Lex? It's only me—only I, I mean! Have you got the nightmare?" "Night*mare?*" cried I. "I thought it was a night-*donkey!*" "And you might have made a bigger mistake," said he.

Now laugh, Nan, my darling, and show your ignorance—of a pun! If I had been coming home I would certainly have brought little

*Long-Ears* with me. He was as gentle as a kitten. One of our men came on here expecting to have some donkeys or *burros* sent after him from Juneau. They didn't come. Our friend got impatient. He telegraphed from Skaguay: "Send on the *bureaus*!" for he didn't know how to spell the word, and went by the sound of it. The operator at the other end was a wag. He wired back: "We haven't got any *bureaus* here, but there's a donkey or two ready to send!" Write me what you think of *that*!

Your cousin,<br>LEX.

In the Skaguay Trail, Alaska,<br>October 2, 1896.

*My Dear Aunt Ellen:*

Lex has just come back from a two days' trip to Skaguay and brought our mail into camp. It was with the greatest delight that we read *your* dear letter, always most welcome, but a hundred times more so now. I only hope you will devote a little spare time very often during the next four months to the same purpose.

As to the hardships we have endured since we left our home in the East, of course they have been a rather distressing experience for two boys reared as tenderly and delicately as we; but we are glad of this severe ordeal. It is gratifying even to ourselves to feel that we have (under God) the manliness and courage to go through all these trials; and the sweetest solace we enjoy in our difficulties is the knowledge that we have in them the sympathy and prayers of the dear ones at home.

We had not the slightest idea that our poor efforts at describing Alaska, and our life in camp, etc., would be so much appreciated. I only wish it were in my power to reproduce to your mind's eye the grandeur and wonderful character of the scenery in every direction from our camp. Looking around you here in this vast solitude it is brought right home to you what a small atom man is on the world's surface. The isolation and the magnificent scenery of gigantic mountain and fathomless abyss bring one very close to God in His sublimest works.

I can assure you, my dear Aunt, that this has

been of the greatest benefit to us both in a spiritual way.

It is like making a grand spiritual Retreat here with Our Lord in the wilderness.

We have been touched to the quick by the description of your recent illness and of the terrible sufferings you have offered up for our welfare and success. Words cannot express our sympathy with you, our gratitude to you for the kind offerings you made of your almost insupportable pains. I trust that the future will prove to you that your prayers have been heard, and that every one of your sufferings has borne heavenly fruit.

To make a change from " grave to gay," I must tell you that our cooking department is rapidly and steadily improving. You would be surprised to see some of the fine pastry I am turning out for my own and Lex's delight.

Many and many a time I have regretted that I did not bring my camera along, as I could have sent some very interesting pictures back to our dear ones.

About two months ago Mr. S. took a snapshot with his camera of Lex and me coming down the mountain side with our *burros*, with packs and pack-saddles. He sent it on to his paper for publication, but I don't know if it ever reached there. Our sturdy little beasts were loaded with our boat in three sections. This was the best-looking feature of the outfit, for, if I remember rightly (you know there are no mirrors *here !*), we boys were hardly presentable. Our clothes, from contact with the rocks, water and mud, made us sorry-looking figures.

But Mr. S. was much elated over the picture; said it was the most typical scene of a mining camp he was able so far to get. I am in doubt as to the exact time it was taken (we are like Robinson Crusoes out here, and are apt to lose all reckonings), or you might get a copy of the paper and see just how it looked.

When we get in, dear Aunt, we shall most certainly look up the priest you speak of, and shall preserve your letter for the purpose of introduction. Many thanks for the suggestion.

It is now twelve o'clock at night. Lex crawled into his sleeping-bag an hour ago; and the wind is howling and snow and sleet are flying in every direction outside our little "shack." I thank God we are housed so snug and warm, and for the time being clear of the exposures of tent-life. As I start at six-thirty to-morrow morning across the mountains to mail this, I shall close, with the hope that we shall have another letter from you in the very near future. God bless you, my dear Aunt, and believe me to be,

Your loving nephew,<br>
LEE.

P.S.—Give mother and the dear girls a good big hug and kiss from their two boys in the polar regions.

Excuse the stationery, etc. I have hard work to keep the pen from going through the paper at every word, but this is considered fine—for up here.

In Winter Quarters,<br>
Twenty Miles from Lake Bennett,<br>
Alaska, Oct. 23, 1896.

*Dear Folks:*

We have an opportunity of sending this off to-morrow by a fellow who is going up and returning. I know you want to know how your two ducks are doing up here in the frozen North. We have built a log cabin ten by twelve, just high enough to stand up comfortably in. We dug it two feet under ground, and then banked it up fully two feet around the base on the outside. We have about two thousand pounds of provisions stacked up in one corner, which we wish to keep untouched for future use. Then we have about five hundred pounds packed up in another corner, which we are now using. We have about 500 lbs. of flour, 200 lbs. of beans, 150 of corn meal, 100 of oatmeal, 100 lbs. of dried fruit, about 50 lbs. of evaporated potatoes, 100 lbs. of bacon, 25 lbs. of coffee, and 20 lbs. of tea, besides butter, crackers, etc., etc. We have four axes, two shovels and two gold-pans.

I would like to send you a sketch of our cabin, if I were artist enough to make it. It would astonish you if you could take a peep into it and see how nearly comfortable (for out here) we have made ourselves. We have manufactured cot-beds out of our discarded tent which had done us such good service before we built our log cabin. Believe me, we considered that we were enjoying a luxury when we lay down on them for the first time. Hitherto we had been obliged to rest on the ground: sometimes with the water running under our backs. Of course we had then a bed made of the boughs and branches of trees. We have a small steel portable heater about one and a half feet square, which has such a draught as to be almost capable of burning cobble stones. We fill this at night before retiring, with green wood, let it start burning until well caught, and then we turn off the draughts and it remains smouldering through the night. When morning comes we turn the draught on by a contrivance of our own invention—(a cord which reaches to our cots), without getting out of our sleeping-bags; and by the time we wish to rise the cabin is most comfortable. I spoke of our sleeping-bags. These to you must be something new, but not to us poor pilgrims out here in the wilderness. Lee and I each have three sleeping-bags apiece, two of which are made out of the heaviest sort of blankets, and over them is placed another very heavy canvas bag. This arrangement keeps us very comfortable at night. Previous to having these bags it seemed impossible for us to keep warm. The mercury has registered about *sixty degrees below* on some few days, but at this season it is generally from twenty-five to thirty-five degrees below. If the north wind is blowing it rushes with such fearful velocity that it makes it seem as cold as at sixty below. It freezes the very breath on your beard (I mean *my* beard, not *yours !*). You will scarcely believe me when I tell you of the amount of clothing which we are obliged to wear. First, we have each a set of the heaviest woollen underwear; next, over that a buckskin suit; next, over that a blue flannel shirt ; then a heavy sweater; then a full suit of canvas lined with sheepskin. Could you imagine any one with such an outfit on at once ? and yet it is not a whit too much, I can assure you. Hoping to hear from you very soon, I am always yours,

LEX.

## XIII.

By this time Aunt Grace's eyes are so full of tears over her boys' hardships that she cannot see to read. She takes off her blurred glasses with a little sob, and wiping them, begins to look around for the twins.

"What *are* those children about?" she exclaims. And she may well ask.

Vaisey and Tasey have long since grown tired of the reading. With Jack and Freddie they have slipped under the netting and taken to playing soldiers over by the Yukon. Jack, having hunted up all the military traps from the tent, has divided the stores, giving Vaisey a drum and Freddie an American flag, but keeping the musket for himself. They have had a drill which would have been delightful if it had not left poor Tasey out in the cold. And now they have just marched to fight for Cuba, when they discover Tasey confiscating the baggage-wagons in revenge. They all pounce down upon the infant Weyler, and then the lookers-on in the Klondike see that Tasey deserves all praise for his ingenuity and grit. He has found two small soap-boxes in the tent, and to each he has harnessed a poodle. In Bute's wagon sits Speckle, reserved and dignified, with all the conscious pride of an F. F. B. In Cute's sits dear big, fluffy, golden Buttercup, whose feathers overflow the box as she clucks contentedly in her chariot. The little teams are so entrancing to behold that Captain Jack's soldiers renounce Cuba on the spot and proceed to make terms with Commissary Tasey. Vaisey drops his drum and seizes Bute's guiding-reins. Tasey grasps Cute's more firmly. The musket and Jack, and the American flag with Fred attached, fall into line, and away goes the triumphant parade.

But alas! and alas! "many a merry going forth maketh a sorrowful coming home." There is a snake in the grass; or, to speak more correctly, there are *two crabs* in the grass—the two live crabs that escaped from the creel some hours back. Do you remember the crawling creatures that got off to the bit of salt marsh when Vaisey poked the seaweed with his stick?

Well, here they are, still wriggling in the grass. There are some cool little hollows in the sand, with a cupful or so of brackish water, and our two hard-shell Baptists have been enjoying their dip all this time and soaking in the shady pools.

Right in their way come the twins with their rival teams. Bute is straining his skin until he looks like an over-boiled pudding. Cute is holding his own with his apoplectic eyes popping out of their sockets. The twins are boldly unsuspecting, and the rear guard audaciously careless. Truth is stranger than fiction, and our readers will scarcely believe that, in less time than it takes to tell it, a crab in ambush has sunk his sharp claws into the plump hind legs of each poodle; and off tears the mad array of dogs, crabs, chickens and twins, yelping, hissing, clucking, and howling like mad. A pack of Eskimo dogs could not make a more heartrending uproar, and the chariot race in "Ben Hur" wouldn't be a snuff to this runaway.

Aunt Grace screams in sympathy, and makes a feeble attempt to follow. But Father Edwards quiets and restrains her.

"Don't worry, Mrs. Kirke," says he with a quiet laugh, "the boys will come out all right—boys always do. If they get a tumble and a scratch or two it won't hurt them. The best men are those who were not coddled when young."

"I'll look after the kids, Aunt Grace," says Herbert, who sees she is still fretting about her babies; and he and Allen and Phil stroll off laughing, to search for the charioteers.

They find them in a very sorry plight.

Vaisey has fallen into Lake Tagish, Tasey into Lake Bennett, and the poodles and the crabs, still closely united, are dragged at last out of Lake Linderman.

It takes a good deal of skill and nerve to restore poor Bute and Cute to the undisputed possession of their wounded hind-legs: but a good-sized stick does the business; and then Speckle and Buttercup are discovered unhurt, taking a sand-bath by the roadside.

"I'm ashamed of you, Jack," says Herbert, with the eldest brother's privilege; "a big, strong fellow like you not able to take better care of these poor little kids!"

"How was I to know that those confounded crabs were in the grass?" grumbles Jack as he helps his brothers to shake and straighten out the twins' clothing and wipe off with his handkerchief the water and sand from their pretty little doleful faces.

"Come along, all of you," orders Bert with dignity. "We've got our camera in the tent, and Father Edwards is going to get it out and take us all in a picture!"

"Hurry up!" cries Phil; and leaving the crabs and the battered baggage-wagons behind them, the runaways pluck up courage and follow their gallant rescuers back to the fairy bower.

Aunt Grace rushes to meet her damaged darlings, catches them up in turn and half smothers them with hugs and kisses before she discovers that their shirt-fronts are wet and their round faces dirty. When off she posts with them to the tent and scrubs them up and combs them down, and with a mother's love and ready tact manages to produce them in a little while clean and dry, and cheerfully prepared for the next adventure, good or bad.

She is just in time to take her place with the twins in the group forming for the picture.

Father Edwards is setting the camera in place, and Miss Elliott is going about among the party putting the sitters into position.

She has arranged Mrs. Arthur Kirke as the central figure, and that lady now makes room beside her for Aunt Grace. Veva and Nan take their places on the right, Jeannie and Olive on the left.

"Nan," says Margaret, "you had better hold Buttercup, and Veva, Speckle. Olive, get your mandolin. Jeannie will do very well with that large garden hat in her hand. Here is a soft rug for Vaisey and Tasey at mamma's feet, and the poodles can curl up there beside them."

"Hadn't Bert better pose with his violin, and

Allen with the banjo?" says Jeannie, as she dangles her great dark hat against the lovely folds of her scarlet organdie.

"Yes," replies the directress; "and if Jack holds the musket, and Fred the drum, Phil may pretend to play on his mouth-organ. Now, back to your places, all of you boys," adds Margaret, "and stand behind the ladies' chairs!"

"Please pose here at the right, Miss Elliott," says the priest, "and have the kindness to tilt this crab-net across your shoulder—so! Attention, little people! One—two—three—ready, all hands!"

In the flash of an eye the thing is done. And well done, too, as it transpires later—save for a mosquito that lights on Philip's nose at the critical moment, making him more cross-eyed than usual, and the broad grin that distorts Jack's face, in consequence, from ear to ear. He has never been "taken" before, and he has vainly expected some one to tell him in advance the precise minute at which to look serious, but the moment has come and gone, leaving behind it a grotesque image of Phil, and an impression of Jack which Miss Elliott dubs in French, "*le garçon qui rit.*"

"The last picture I made," says Father Edwards, after laying aside the photograph for future development, "was that of little Raymond Stanhope. Dear little Raymond Stanhope!" and the priest's fine eyes grow misty and full of dreamy thought.

"Is he dead?" question the girls with interest.

"I know not if he be dead or alive," is the reply; "yet I trust God has him in His keeping wherever he may be. Let me tell you about him," says Father Edwards, seating himself before them. "When I was an assistant on my first mission I had charge of a select school for young boys taught by the good Sisters of Mercy. The first time I visited the classes Sister Innocentia pointed out to me a little boy of seven who had just entered the school. He was not what is called a pretty child, but his face was bright and earnest. His golden hair, soft and silky, fell in love-locks around his face and in thick, waving curls upon his shoulders. His little form, straight as an arrow, was set off to the best advantage by a dainty jacket and knickerbockers of black velvet, with a big white lace collar and wrist-ruffles. His name was Raymond Stanhope, and the previous summer vacation he had spent in Europe with his parents, whose only child he was. In England, and also on the voyage, he had been praised and petted as a genuine little *Lord Fauntleroy.* 'Indeed,' said Sister Innocentia, ' every visitor to the school exclaims at seeing him: "There is *little Lord Fauntleroy!*" One might expect to find him a spoiled child,' the Sister went on to say, ' but he is nothing of the sort. He is a faithful little scholar, always eager with offers of service in small ways, before and after school. He is especially attentive to religious instruction, and last week, when the children who have not yet been admitted to holy communion, made their quarterly confession, Raymond paid the strictest attention to all that was said to prepare him for that Holy Sacrament, and asked questions of Sister which showed the careful devotion of his heart. Last spring,' continued Sister Innocentia, ' his parents took him to Washington to witness the inauguration of President Harrison. After that ceremony the Stanhopes were introduced to the President, when he placed his hand on Raymond's head and expressed the hope that the little boy would grow up into a good man, and that God would always bless him. It was after the return of the party from Washington that Mother Francis began the instructions for the June confessions. Raymond was most attentive. He had a cousin two or three years older than he. He was motherless, and very delicate, and a public school pupil. Raymond watched over this child with great care, and sometimes brought him with him to our school. A little while before the June confessions Raymond asked Mother Francis if his cousin might not come and receive instructions with the others. Mother replied that she feared our children were too far advanced for him, and that he had better wait until the next time—three months from that date. Raymond went back to his seat, but Mother saw that he was uneasy, that his mind was taken up with the thought of his cousin. Several times afterwards he returned to the subject, and asked permission to bring the stranger-boy to the instructions. Each time it grew harder for Mother Francis to say that he had better wait. At last one day the brave little fellow marched up to Mother's desk in school hours, and looking gravely at her with his clear, bright eyes, said: " Can nothing be done for my cousin, Mother Francis?" This settled it,' said Sister Innocentia. 'Although the child did not belong to our school, and the confession did not seem necessary, Mother told Raymond to bring him down to the convent after school each evening and she would prepare him for the sacrament. This our little Lord Fauntleroy did with a joy and diligence that were absolutely admirable to behold. He would wait each day in the yard, or in his seat in the class-room, until his cousin was through with the instructions, and then they would run off home happily together. The invalid cousin made his confession, and, strange to say, only a few days after was found in a fit one morning in his bed. He never recovered from that convulsion. It ended his little life in two or three hours. Mother Francis and the Sisters were all deeply moved by this incident. They began to look upon Raymond almost with reverence, for God had made use of that dear, sweet child as the instrument of His grace to the soul of the dead boy. Is it not lovely, Father,' concluded Sister Innocentia— ' is it not lovely to know that Raymond Stanhope will carry with him his whole life long the grace of his cousin's prayers ? ' "

There is a brief silence. Father Edwards gazes out over the sea with the same dreamy look he wore when he first mentioned Raymond's name. Tears are in the eyes of the girls. Even the boys are moved by the story; but they do not want to show it.

At a signal from Mrs. Arthur Kirke the musical instruments all sound forth in sweet harmony, and the children rejoice to sing together their May hymn to OUR LADY OF LIGHT:

"When the clouds of sin, obscuring,
  O'er our pathway meet,
When temptation's snares, alluring,
  Darken round our feet,

If we pray thee, Mother tender,
  Ever near, thou art;
Cloud and snare thou turns't to splendor,
  Sunshine of the heart!

"When the shadows of affliction
  All our hopes destroy,
And we miss the benediction
  Of a by-gone joy;
Mother, round thy feet we cluster
  Till the shades depart;
Grief is lost in thy fair lustre,
  Sunshine of the heart!"

## XIV.

TEA having been made by Miss Elliott and handed around by Veva and Nan, Vaisey falls asleep in Jeannie's lap, and Tasey, in Olive's. The great heat of the day is over. A delicious breeze blows from the sea, and sweet peace descends, like a gentle dew, upon all our hot and tired picnickers.

"Before our Klondike picnic is at an end," says Father Edwards, "please let us hear the conclusion of the Alaskan letters."

And Aunt Grace, drawing forth from her bag for the third and last time the precious packet, gives a tender, motherly glance at her sleeping twins and begins again to read the records of the gold-seekers of the Skaguay.

Skaguay, Alaska,<br>Oct. 26, 1896.

*My Dear Cousin Margaret:*

I came over the mountain day before yesterday to get my mail and to answer letters from mother and Veva, also from Aunt Nellie, intending to return early this morning; but on awakening we found it impossible to cross the summit, owing to a blizzard having sprung up during the night; luckily this delayed me until the arrival of the little steamer *Alki* from Juneau, with your welcome letters on board, also books and papers which, my dear cousin, I assure you, are veritable godsends, as those are articles which we rarely see out in this wilderness.

Why, you dear Madge, I would give the world, almost, were you with us, more especially for your cheery good-humor and your "fancy cooking." You would be surprised, though, to find how it brings one out in this line (not meaning "to blow my own horn"). I'm becoming quite a cook; but in point of fact, life in this wilderness brings one out in many ways, as you must depend entirely upon your own resources, and it's surprising how often they are called upon. So far we have providentially surmounted them all; but we cannot, at this writing, count on the future. Up to the present time, however, as I say, we have held our end up with the hardiest of them.

There were two women started in over this trail. Of course they carried nothing, having plenty of money (their intention being to start a bank at Dawson City), but they soon gave up and returned to Chicago. It was foolish for them to start.

We have every hope in the world of making a rich strike when we reach the gold fields; as we hear occasionally of wonderful finds in every direction. There isn't the slightest doubt of this whole country being full of *gold*, but, Great Scott ! it's hard to get back at it.

It seems so aggravating to know that, had we not had to pack our two tons of provisions, etc., with us we could have been in the mines two months ago; and yet to go without them was certain death.

There isn't the slightest doubt but what they are starving in Dawson to-day, as they have been utterly unable to get provisions there; but I suppose the papers give you this information.

Your calendar came in like an angel of comfort, for it's something we have wanted for a long time. We often fail to know the day of the week, and often have a discussion as to the day of the month. I think this is dated somewhere within a day or two of the right time.

It seems funny to hear you mention "*wheels.*" Why, I had almost forgotten what a bicycle looks like; but my! wouldn't I enjoy a good ride through the Park?

We look forward to going home in the near future with a big strike. What a wonderful thing is money! We have seen men in this trail who, when they arrived, looked like gentlemen; but oh! in about a week they developed into downright brutes in their struggle to reach the Land of Promise, caring for nothing, themselves included, until one begins to think that human life is at a discount. Why, it has been quite an ordinary thing to see men lie right down to sleep on the rocks in the rain after having put their horses in their tents, because the horse would die of exposure! Poor, deluded fellows! some have been obliged to go back complete wrecks, who, on their first coming, were in perfect health. Others, again, would really amuse you—fellows out with a pack of perhaps thirty to forty pounds, men who have never before carried a bundle. They go the first three miles, pretty level, strike the foot of the first mountain, perhaps go up a couple of hundred yards, look up at the top (one thousand feet away, maybe), sit down on a rock, and finally throw the pack in the trail, and—off they go. You never see them again, as they return disgusted to civilization. There are many funny things occurring, if one were not too tired to appreciate them.

Now, my dear, I trust you will drop us a line as often as possible; even if we do not get the letters for several weeks, they are worth their weight in gold when they *do* come.

Kindest regards to all.
Yours,
LEE.

P.S.—We had a sick man staying with us a few nights ago, completely used up with overwork and coarse food. We met him on the steamer coming up, and a finer-looking fellow you never saw. When he struck our cabin the other night, he was a wreck—literally fell into the door. He had walked all the way from the summit. His partner was with him—a doctor—and he was taking him back to New York *via* Skaguay. The poor fellow had told him on the summit that if he could only get to our shack he knew we would take care of him. The worst of it is, he thinks he is going to get well East, and then return here in the spring. But the doctor says his lungs are affected, and he'll never come back to the Klondike again. He'll go a longer and a sadder journey. Pray for us all! These experiences show us how uncertain life is, and how forlorn a place this is to be sick and die in.

Camp Emergency, Skaguay Trail,<br>Alaska, Nov. 26, 1896.

*Dearest Mother and Folks:*

We cannot tell you with what joy we received and read your letters from "home, sweet home." We have read them over and over again until we know them by heart. We are fourteen miles from Skaguay. Just think how much we must long to hear from you all, when we walk that distance back and forth, through fourteen miles of horrible mud, dead horses, rapids and precipices (it takes two days in all), to get your letters and to send our answers! The mail charges are very high here; there is no U. S. Post-office here yet, although one has been arranged for. The man who is running the mail office now charges five cents extra on every letter coming in and going out, which is pretty expensive for poor men. When we first came through Skaguay in September it was a city of tents. Now the town is quite built up—whole streets of houses, theatres, saloons, gambling dens—everything, alas! but—*churches*.

I will mail this to you to-morrow, as I have to go over to Skaguay then to buy some tar-paper to line the roof of our cabin with. We found it leaking badly during a heavy rain when we wakened in the middle of the night; and what was worse, we just had to grin and bear it, as we had nothing available with which to stop the leak.

Since writing the above I was obliged to stop, and I now resume my letter. We have been to Skaguay and back, but I assure you I do not want such a journey again, for a while at least. When returning, darkness overtook us, and for several hours we were forced to plough our way over this most terrible Pass, scarcely able to see our hand before us. More terrible still, we heard that day that three enormous grizzly bears had been seen on the trail. You will believe me when I tell you we were two of the *deadest* fellows you ever saw by the time we reached our shack (that is what they call the cabin out here). These grizzly bears of which I speak are so ferocious that even the old hunters will not hunt them. You can imagine our feelings when we were groping our way in the darkness, with the dread of meeting these monsters. At times we would be knee-deep in mud, then over rocks and then through water, etc. I will be willing to swear that never again will we be caught in such a fix. We expect to remain here until some time in February, when the ice is so firm that it will bear a yoke of oxen. We will then start over the lakes. We look back now at the terrible experience of the past, and it seems to us like some dreadful nightmare. The dangers and terrors through which we have been obliged to travel have made us blind to the superb grandeur of the scenery. We have been obliged to keep our eyes and ears glued to this frightful trail, where one misstep meant either to break an arm or a leg, or even worse—to be hurled to a cruel death! We have, however, survived it all, through the mercy of God. And we trust in Him to extend the same merciful care over us in our future trials. You cannot, by any stretch of your imagination, realize what a trip through this vast wilderness means. Climb one of these mountains as we have done, twelve thousand feet high, starting at the base: first through heavy underbrush, jumping from rock to rock at an angle of sixty degrees, for perhaps one thousand feet, to timber line; then up an almost perpendicular rock-slide, skirting precipices, mountain torrents, over the rocks, with a soft bed of moss perhaps eight to ten feet deep; thence to the summit—a trip consuming from four to six hours, part of which you are sometimes passing through snow up to your waist. Then you look around you and see what a view you behold! Mountains, mountains, mountains on all sides—some running up to the clouds; snow-storms raging wherever you turn. We thought when we reached the summit of the one on which we stood that we had gotten to the top of it; but we found that we had only *commenced* to ascend. I assure you, such a situation as this makes you realize what an atom you are in God's creation.

To change the subject, I must tell you that we have learned something about cooking since you last saw us. It would surprise you could you but see the fine apple, peach, plum and raisin pies that I can now make. Also, I am quite proficient in cooking Boston baked beans, to say nothing of the fine buckwheat cakes which we make (and put away any quantity of), covered with maple syrup. We are, however, forced to be very saving of our stuff, as we do not know what emergency may be forthcoming. We have with us a doctor from the state of Washington, who will start with us over the lakes in February, and who has friends already out on the Stewart River. They report a fabulous find there. Let us hope that such luck is awaiting *us*, and be sure that if such is the case you, my dear ones, will be the first to hear of it.

Hoping to get some letters from you when I go over to Skaguay to mail this, I am, as always,

Yours affectionately,
LEX.

## XV.

In the Skaguay Trail, Alaska,
December 1, 1896.

*Dear Uncle Arthur:*

We are quite comfortable in our shack. It is a dandy place compared to a tent. The last camping-place we had before we built our cabin was on a large flat rock about three feet above the river, with nice dry sand, like seashore sand. We thought it was elegant; but the day after we got everything fixed it started in for a three or four days' steady rain. The consequence was we were routed out at midnight with the river running up over our rock. The water was three feet deep over it before another day was past. It was no fun to have to pull up stakes and hunt a new camp at twelve o'clock at night, and it raining like smoke. But such is life in this glorious land of Alaska.

We are chafing every day that goes by at the unavoidable delay caused by the conditions of the trail. You can form no idea of what a wild, weird and barren country this part of the globe is; and a man must needs keep all his wits about him, and exercise good judgment, or he may be led into the greatest dangers and difficulties. Your outfit of food and clothing is worth everything to you—money scarcely anything. We realized this long ago, and have profited by it. We are now housed very comfortably (for here) and have a very good outfit, which will last us, with care, until we start in over the ice about February 1st, and leave us enough for one year's prospecting.

It is pitiable to see the numbers who have turned back, disheartened, disgusted, and penniless; and the trail is strewn with abandoned provisions of all kinds, most of it utterly ruined, lying just where it has been thrown. Yet the feeling seems so strong against any one touching another man's outfit, that stuff that could be utilized you dare not take lest the owner may come back looking for it in the spring. There are quite a number of men who have gone back to their homes with the intention of coming up in the spring, having put their outfits in a *cache;* but a trip over the trail as far as the summit will easily show one how vain the hope is to ever locate these goods again. The snow, even at this early date, has, in most cases, obliterated all signs of where they are. It is figured here that at least one million dollars has been thrown away this fall on this trail alone, in provisions, horses, and labor, in the effort to reach the gold fields. Of the very few who have started down the lakes (as far as we can find out here), about two hundred must have been wrecked at White Horse Rapids (the most dangerous trip), or have been compelled to abandon the most of their outfits, working for Dawson City, with possibly one hundred and fifty to three hundred pounds of provisions, to take their chances of starvation and the black vomit (which is another terror they are likely to have added to their troubles). So we content ourselves as best we can with our delay here, and feel that we have used good judgment.

The other day was Lex's birthday, so we thought we'd have a "spread." We asked in a few of the fellows, and here is the dinner I cooked, and Lex set before them. Talk about your Paris cooking after this! It was a course dinner—ahem!

MÉNU KLONDIKE.
Bean Soup (nary Slouch).
Fresh Baked Salmon (à la Frenchie).
Roast Grouse (à la Samee).
Fried Potatoes (à la Onions).
Baked Beans (à la Boston).

| *Bread.* | *Pies.* |
|---|---|
| Pop-overs (Wheat). | Apple. |
| Biscuits (Graham). | Peach. |

Cheese.   Coffee and Tea.

Wasn't that a royal lay-out? We drank all your healths in coffee, and then told yarns till our lamp went out.

We intend going right at mining as soon as we reach our destination. We feel fully able to do this, as we are both, to use a common expression, as hard as nails. You will be surprised to hear it, but it is a fact that seven-tenths of the men who quit and went back, were men who in the East were used to hard work. We expect to lay up here until about the middle of February, when they say the storms on the summit cease. We will then take up the march on sleighs. The snow on the summit at present is six feet deep, and snowing every day, with a regular gale of wind going all the while. The weather here in the mountains, about eight miles from the foot of the summit, is not so severe, as we have only about two and a half feet of snow at present, and the mercury has not gone below zero yet. It averages about one or two degrees above.

We keep pretty actively employed chopping firewood, of which I guess you know by experience with Western climates it takes quantities. But we built our cabin with a low roof (just room enough to clear our heads), and two feet of the cabin itself is under ground. We then banked it on the outside a couple of feet, so that we keep pretty comfortable.

The days are now getting very short. We don't see the sun until after ten o'clock, and it is gone by two-thirty. It seems very odd to look at it at twelve o'clock, noon, away down in the south, instead of overhead.

Write to us as often as you can, and we shall be glad to reply whenever we get the chance.

Faithfully your nephew,
LEE.

Camp Emergency, Skaguay Trail,<br>Alaska, Dec. 15, 1896.

*Dearest Mother and Folks:*

Your last letters were received with greatest joy. You cannot imagine what they are to us out here in this wilderness. I hope you got the photo we sent you last time we wrote. In it you will see your two beauties standing one on each side of our cabin. The one with the axe is me, the one with the gun is Lee. Can you make them out? Pretty hard-looking fellows to meet on a lonely road—aren't we? You will be surprised to learn that since writing you last we have taken a contract (in combination with another fellow) to put up a cabin for a man out here. We built it about twice the size of ours. He paid us well for it, and we were very glad to have something to do that kept us hardened up for our expected trip across the lakes in February. It was, however, very cold work, as the mercury then ranged along about from fifteen to twenty-five degrees below zero. The north wind comes sometimes like a cyclone, and will blow in this way for two or three weeks at a time. We are, however, acclimated, and are besides clothed very warmly, with large fur caps which almost completely cover our heads and faces, so that we stand it amazingly well. Some weeks ago we went up over the mountains to the right of the cabin (you see them in the picture). It was a hunting trip for bear and wild goats. There were four of us in the party. It took us six hours to get to the top. Then we went down into a valley where we pitched a camp, intending to stay three or four days; but the night we got there it started in a regular blizzard—snowed all night hard, and looked as if it would keep up for a week. So we broke camp, and hustled back through three feet of snow; and it was no picnic, I tell you. We didn't get any fresh meat, but we had a good tramp, and felt jolly over it. It put me in mind of the old nursery rhyme about the men marching up the hill and then marching down again. I forgot to tell you that the chief house in Skaguay, and the one which is used as a post-office, is called the "Holly House." It is kept by a young fellow named Sarpotius, from New York; I believe he was one of the Four Hundred.

This is a miserable, lonesome country. We would not think this to be so if we could only keep moving; but the delay of this long wait before travelling on again is very wearisome. We learn from parties coming out from Dawson City that they are having a fearful time there. Fevers, scurvy and starvation are carrying off numbers. We are glad that we did not succeed in reaching there, as I have no doubt we would have been deprived of our provisions, after all we had suffered to bring them thus far. Continue to pray for us. Hoping to hear from you very soon, I am, with love to all,

Yours affectionately,<br>
LEX.

## XVI.

Camp Emergency, Skaguay Trail,
Alaska, Dec. 18, 1896.

*Dear Mother and Folks:*

Since writing you last we have had cause to change our plans altogether in regard to remaining here in our shack until February. A couple of days ago, just after our last letter to you, we entertained the captain of the Canadian Mounted Police and the head of the Customs' duties at Lake Tagish. He stayed with us over night, and he tells us that out of the thousands moving towards Alaska, hundreds are arriving at Skaguay. He advises us, therefore, to lose no more time now, but to start at once over the ice and snow. He says that we may be caught in a mighty crush if we wait longer. So by the time this reaches you we will have commenced our travels over the lakes, with our outfits packed on sleds. The duties on these goods are enormous, being forty per cent. We are obliged to pay the Canadian Government half as much in duty as the goods cost originally. We will write you at the first opportunity we get; but I would advise that you do not write again to us until you hear from us. We have secured some very valuable information as to where it is best to prospect first, and just as soon as we find our hopes are confirmed we will get you word in some way or other. As we will be obliged to keep moving steadily, we do not expect to pitch our tent at night, but think we will have to lie right on top of the snow, with camp-fires around us, each taking his turn as night-watch, to keep the fires going. Ice is six feet deep on the rivers, snow four feet deep. Good-by and God bless you! We have a party of eight with us. Pray hard for our safety and success!

P.S.—By the middle of February or the 1st of March the snow will have such a crust on it that we can drive a team of horses over it, they tell us. The blizzards will be over by that time. We keep wonderfully well. If one's lungs are all O. K. this is the banner place of the world for building up a constitution. All the same, when we once get what we are after, no one will be quicker or gladder to jump back to civilized life than,

Yours lovingly,<br>
LEX and LEE.

\* \* \* \*

As Aunt Grace finishes the last letter she begins to sob pitifully:

"*That*," she murmurs, "was written last December, and it is now May—five long months—and not a line since! Oh, who can say whether my darling boys ever reached the gold-fields! Who, except God, knows whether they are now alive or dead?"

She covers her face with her handkerchief and rocks to and fro, moaning softly to herself.

"Courage, dear Grace!" whispers Mrs. Arthur Kirke, "and put your trust firmly in God. Not one of His creatures can ever wander so far away as to get outside the circle of His divine care and providence."

"Let us hope," says Father Edwards, with his kindly smile, "that Lex and Lee are safe and well in camp at Stewart River. At this very moment, Mrs. Kirke, a message from them may be speeding towards you."

"Alas!" sighs Aunt Grace, "I feel sure I shall never hear from them again. Only yesterday I saw in the *Press* that two miners were found dead at Stewart River, after having dug out nearly two hundred thousand dollars in nuggets. Their names were not known, but their frozen bodies were brought into Skaguay strapped to a sled. Ever since I read it, I have firmly believed those men to be my own darling Lex and Lee!" and again she broke down into tears.

"Don't ky, mamma! don't ky!" cry the heavenly twins in chorus; and in a moment Vaisey has his plump arms around Aunt Grace's neck, while Tasey clasps her knees; and both start to howl like little prairie wolves: "Ooze dot *us*, anyhow, mamma! ooze dot *us*, and us won't doe to any nasty 'Laska to die!"

Aunt Grace hugs them close to her, and begins to smile through her tears. Father Edwards draws out his watch and looks at it.

"It is now five o'clock," he remarks, "and if we want to get back to Shell Beach in time for our May devotions I think we had better be on the move."

Immediately all is excitement and bustle—breaking camp. The boys and girls run hither and thither, gathering up and storing away in the tent mosquito-netting, table, camp-chairs, musical instruments, crab-nets, fishing lines, camera, and all the "properties" of a Klondike picnic.

Everything is made safe and taut. Hats are tied on, caps adjusted, empty baskets caught up with many a laugh and joke upon their lightness.

Father Edwards leads the way to the landing. The sunburned boys and girls follow in his track, shouting, telling merry stories, or giving out funny riddles. Mrs. Arthur Kirke brings up the rear, supporting upon her arm poor, sad-hearted Aunt Grace. The twins are close at their heels, with their body-guard of poodles and chickens.

Margaret whispers to Veva and Jeannie:

"I am really afraid, girls, that if Aunt Grace does not hear soon from Lex and Lee she will die of pure grief. She has broken dreadfully the past three months!"

"Hark!" cries Veva, "they are beginning to sing the evening hymn to the Sacred Heart!"

And as they travel on to the pier, the children, led by Father Edwards' clear, strong tenor, are heard chanting sweetly, with a fine echo from the cliffs:

"When all the day of toil is done
   And twilight spreads her purple wing,
When starry vigils have begun
   Before the Eucharistic King—
As earth's poor lovers at the tryst,
   Impassion'd, to the lov'd one flee,
O true and tender Heart of Christ,
   We haste to give the night to Thee!

"In joy or grief, in hope or fear,
   In sin, in suff'ring, and distress,
Behold a Refuge ever near—
   To heal, to comfort, and to bless.
In light or darkness, life and death,
   In time and in eternity,
Devoted Heart, with trusting faith
   We consecrate our all to Thee!"

"To Thee—to Thee—to Thee—our all to

Thee!" the echoes sing among the moss-crowned rocks, as if the guardian spirits of the island were joining with the innocent children in paying homage and praise to the great Heart of their Creator.

"It is like the evening echoes of the Alps," says Father Edwards. "When the herdsmen chant at sunset, 'Praise God, all ye creatures, praise God!' the mighty mountains send back the echo of the prayer from a hundred snowy peaks: 'Praise God! praise God!'"

"There comes old Saltee in his boat!" cries Philip over his shoulder, as the pretty sail-boat comes in sight approaching the pier, airy and graceful against the blue waters as a white-winged bird against the blue expanse of heaven.

"And oh! see, see!" shout Nan and Veva joyfully, "papa is on board! He has come to meet us!"

The boat is now close enough for all to see a tall, stout, fair-haired gentleman in the prow, who lifts his hat smilingly and waves it over his head.

He is the only passenger, it being Captain Saltee's last trip for the day.

"Strange that he should have come!" whispers Mrs. Kirke to Aunt Grace. "I did not expect him. He must have been so tired after his long, hot day in the city."

By this time Mr. Arthur Kirke has leaped upon the pier, has saluted Father Edwards, kissed his daughters and Philip, and now comes forward to press his lips upon his wife's cheek.

But it is before Aunt Grace that he makes the longest pause.

He looks at her wistfully, steadily, for a few moments, and his manly cheek changes color.

His face is very pale as he puts a yellow envelope into her hand, saying:

"As I passed the telegraph office a while ago the messenger gave me this dispatch for you!"

She takes it from him like a woman in a dream.

Her face has grown even paler than his own. Her large, dark eyes have a queer, strained look in them—a frightened, hunted look, like those of a fawn at bay. She tries to moisten her dry lips, but her voice is dreary with despair :

"It is to tell me that Lex and Lee are dead ! They are dead, Arthur—dead—dead—dead !"

Then she tears open the envelope, reads with greedy haste the words upon the yellow slip, and with a shriek she falls down among them all in a death-like swoon.

The twins scream, Captain Saltee runs for fresh water, Miss Elliott snatches her smelling-salts from her bag. The boys and girls crowd around, but Mr. Kirke has stooped and picked up the fatal message. His wife looks over his shoulder, a great brightness shining in her face.

"Thank God !" she sobs, "thank God for all His mercies ! Read it to them, Arthur, read it !"

And just as Aunt Grace sits up in Margaret's arms Mr. Kirke reads aloud to the eager group the long-expected telegram from Juneau:

"*We have struck it rich at last ! We are well and happy, and will start for home to-morrow !*
LEX and LEE."

PRINTED BY BENZIGER BROTHERS, NEW YORK.

# STANDARD CATHOLIC BOOKS

PUBLISHED BY

## BENZIGER BROTHERS,

| CINCINNATI, | NEW YORK: | CHICAGO: |
|---|---|---|
| 343 Main St. | 86 & 38 BARCLAY ST. | 178 Monroe St. |

ABANDONMENT; or, Absolute Surrender of Self to Divine Providence. By Rev. J P. CAUSSADE, S.J. 32mo, *net*, 0 40

ALTAR BOY'S MANUAL, LITTLE. Illustrated. 32mo, 0 25

ANALYSIS OF THE GOSPELS of the Sundays of the Year. By Rev. L. A. LAMBERT, LL.D. 12mo, *net*, 1 25

ART OF PROFITING BY OUR FAULTS, according to St. Francis de Sales. By Rev. J. TISSOT. 32mo, *net*, 0 40

BIBLE, THE HOLY. With Annotations, References, and an Historical and Chronological Index. 12mo, cloth, ? 25

BIRTHDAY SOUVENIR, OR DIARY. With a Subject of Meditation for Every Day. By Mrs. A. E. BUCHANAN. 32mo, 0 50

BLESSED ONES OF 1888. 16mo, illustrated, 0 50

BLIND FRIEND OF THE POOR: Reminiscences of the Life and Works of Mgr. DE SEGUR. 16mo, 0 50

BLISSYLVANIA POST-OFFICE, THE. By MARION AMES TAGGART. 16mo, 0 50

BONE RULES; or, Skeleton of English Grammar. By Rev. J. B. Tabb. 16mo, *net*, 0 35

BOYS' AND GIRLS' MISSION BOOK. By the Redemptorist Fathers. 48mo, 0 35

BOYS' AND GIRLS' ANNUAL. 0 05

BROWNSON, ORESTES A., Literary, Scientific, and Political Views of. Selected from his works. 12mo, *net*, 1 25

BUGG, LELIA HARDIN. Correct Thing for Catholics. 16mo, 0 75

———— A Lady. Manners and Social Usages. 16mo, 1 00

BY BRANSCOME RIVER. By M. A. Taggart. 16mo, 0 50

CANTATA CATHOLICA. Containing a large collection of Masses, etc. HELLEBUSCH. Oblong 4to, *net*, 2 00

CATECHISM OF FAMILIAR THINGS. Their History and the Events which led to their Discovery. 12mo, illustrated, 1 00

CATHOLIC BELIEF; or, a Short and Simple Exposition of Catholic Doctrine. By the Very Rev. JOSEPH FAÀ DI BRUNO, D.D. 200th Thousand. 16mo.
    Paper, 0.25; 25 copies, 4.25; 50 copies, 7.50; 100 copies, 12 50
    Cloth, 0.50; 25 copies, 8.50; 50 copies, 15.00; 100 copies, 25 00

"The amount of good accomplished by it can never be told."—*Catholic Union and Times.*

CATHOLIC CEREMONIES and Explanation of the Ecclesiastical Year. By the Abbé Durand. With 96 illustrations. 24mo.
Paper, 0.25; 25 cop., 4.25; 50 cop., 7.50; 100 cop., 12 50
Cloth, 0.50; 25 cop., 8.50; 50 cop., 15.00; 100 cop., 25 00
A practical, handy volume for the people at a low price. It has been highly recommended by Cardinals, Archbishops, and Bishops

CATHOLIC FAMILY LIBRARY. Composed of "The Christian Father," "The Christian Mother," "Sure Way to a Happy Marriage," "Instructions on the Commandments and Sacraments," and "Stories for First Communicants." 5 volumes in box, 2 00

CATHOLIC HOME ANNUAL. 0 25

CATHOLIC HOME LIBRARY. 10 volumes. 12mo, each, 0 45
Per Set, 3 00

CATHOLIC WORSHIP. The Sacraments, Ceremonies, and Festivals of the Church Explained. Brennan. Paper, 0.15; per 100, 9.00. Cloth, 0.25; per 100, 15 00

CATHOLIC YOUNG MAN OF THE PRESENT DAY. By Right Rev. Augustine Egger, D.D. 32mo, cloth, 0.25; per 100, 15 00

CHARITY THE ORIGIN OF EVERY BLESSING. 16mo, 0 75

CHILD OF MARY. A complete Prayer-Book for Children of Mary. 32mo, 0 60

CHRIST IN TYPE AND PROPHECY. By Rev. A. J. Maas, S.J. 2 vols., 12mo, *net*, 4 00

CHRISTIAN ANTHROPOLOGY. By Rev. J. Thein. 8vo, *net*, 2 50

CHRISTIAN FATHER, THE: What he Should be, and What he Should Do. Paper, 0.25; per 100, 12.50. Cloth, 0.35; per 100, 21 00

CHRISTIAN MOTHER, THE: the Education of her Children and her Prayer. Paper, 0.25; per 100, 12.50. Cloth, 0.35; per 100, 21 00

CIRCUS-RIDER'S DAUGHTER, THE. A novel. By F. v. Brackel. 12mo, 1 25

CLARKE, REV. RICHARD F., S.J. The Devout Year. Short Meditations. 24mo, *net*, 0 60

COBBETT, W. History of the Protestant Reformation. New Edition with Notes and Preface, by Very Rev. F. A. Gasquet, D.D., O.S.B., 12mo, cloth, *net*, 0 50

COMEDY OF ENGLISH PROTESTANTISM, THE. Edited by A. F. Marshall, B.A. Oxon. 12mo, *net*, 0 50

COMPENDIUM SACRAE LITURGIAE Juxta Ritum Romanum una cum Appendice De Jure Ecclesiastico Particulari in America Foederata Sept. vigente scripsit P. Wapelhorst, O.S.F. 8vo, *net*, 2 50

CONFESSIONAL, THE. By Right Rev. A. Roegel, D.D. Translated by Rev. Augustine Wirth, O.S.B. 12mo, *net*, 1 00

2

CONNOR D'ARCY'S STRUGGLES. A novel. By Mrs. W. M. BERTHOLDS. 12mo, 1 25

COUNSELS OF A CATHOLIC MOTHER to Her Daughter. 16mo, 0 50

CROWN OF MARY. THE. A Complete Manual of Devotion for Clients of the Blessed Virgin. 32mo, 0 60

CROWN OF THORNS, THE; or, The Little Breviary of the Holy Face. 32mo, 0 50

DATA OF MODERN ETHICS EXAMINED, THE. By Rev. JOHN J. MING, S.J. 12mo, *net*, 2 00

DE GOESBRIAND, RIGHT REV. L. Christ on the Altar. 4to, richly illustrated, gilt edges, 6 00
—— Jesus the Good Shepherd. 16mo, *net*, 0 75
—— The Labors of the Apostles. 12mo, *net*, 1 00

DEVOTIONS AND PRAYERS BY ST. ALPHONSUS. A Complete Prayer-Book. 16mo, 1 00

EGAN, MAURICE F. The Vocation of Edward Conway. A novel. 12mo, 1 25
—— Flower of the Flock, and Badgers of Belmont. 12mo, 1 00
—— How They Worked Their Way, and Other Stories, 1 00
—— The Boys in the Block. 24mo, leatherette, 0 25
—— A Gentleman. 16mo, 0 75

ENGLISH READER. By Rev. EDWARD CONNOLLY, S.J. 12mo, 1 25

EPISTLES AND GOSPELS. 32mo, 0 25

EUCHARISTIC CHRIST, THE. Reflections and Considerations on the Blessed Sacrament. By Rev. A. TESNIERE. 12mo, *net*, 1 00

EUCHARISTIC GEMS. A Thought about the Most Blessed Sacrament for Every Day. By Rev. L. C. COELENBIER. 16mo, 0 75

EXAMINATION OF CONSCIENCE for the use of Priests who are Making a Retreat. By GADUEL. 32mo, *net*, 0 30

EXPLANATION OF THE BALTIMORE CATECHISM of Christian Doctrine. By Rev. THOMAS L. KINKEAD. 12mo, *net*, 1 00

EXPLANATION OF THE COMMANDMENTS, ILLUSTRATED. By Rev. H. ROLFUS, D.D. With a Practice and Reflection on each Commandment, by Very Rev. F. GIRARDEY, C.SS.R. 16mo, 0 75

This is a very interesting and instructive explanation of the Commandments of God and of the Church, with numerous examples, anecdotes, Scripture passages, etc.

EXPLANATION OF THE GOSPELS, and Explanation of Catholic Worship. 24mo, illustrated.
Paper, 0.25; 25 copies, 4.25; 50 copies, 7.50; 100 copies, 12 50
Cloth, 0.50; 25 copies, 8.50; 50 copies, 15.00; 100 copies, 25 00

EXPLANATION OF THE MASS. By Father VON COCHEM. Preface by Bishop MAES. 12mo, 1 25

EXPLANATION OF THE OUR FATHER AND THE HAIL MARY. Adapted by Rev. RICHARD BRENNAN, LL.D. 16mo, 0 75

EXPLANATION OF THE SALVE REGINA. By St. ALPHONSUS LIGUORI. 16mo, 0 75

**EXPLANATION OF THE PRAYERS AND CEREMONIES OF THE MASS, ILLUSTRATED.** By Rev. I. D. LANSLOTS, O.S.B. With 22 full-page illustrations. 12mo, 1 25
  Clearly explains the meaning of the altar, of its ornaments, of the vestments, of the prayers, and of the ceremonies performed by the celebrant and his ministers.

**EXTREME UNCTION.** Paper, 10 cents; per 100, 5 00
  The same in German at the same prices.

**FABIOLA;** or, The Church of the Catacombs. By CARDINAL WISEMAN. Illustrated Edition. 12mo, 1 25
  Edition de luxe, 6 00

**FATAL DIAMONDS, THE.** By ELEANOR C. DONNELLY. 24mo, fancy leatherette binding, 0 25

**FINN, REV. FRANCIS J., S.J.** Percy Wynn; or, Making a Boy of Him. 12mo, 0 85
———— Tom Playfair; or, Making a Start. 12mo, 0 85
———— Harry Dee; or, Working it Out. 12mo, 0 85
———— Claude Lightfoot; or, How the Problem was Solved. 12mo, 0 85
———— Ethelred Preston; or, The Adventures of a Newcomer. 12mo, 0 85
———— That Football Game, and What Came of It. 12mo, 0 85
———— Mostly Boys. 16mo, 0 85
———— My Strange Friend. 24mo, leatherette, 0 25

**FIRST COMMUNICANT'S MANUAL.** Small 32mo, 0 50

**FIVE O'CLOCK STORIES;** or, The Old Tales Told Again. 16mo, 0 75

**FLOWERS OF THE PASSION.** Thoughts of St. Paul of the Cross. By Rev. LOUIS TH. DE JÉSUS-AGONISANT. 32mo, 0 50

**FOLLOWING OF CHRIST, THE.** By THOMAS À KEMPIS.
  With reflections. Small 32mo, cloth, 0 50
  Without reflections. Small 32mo, cloth, 0 45
  Edition de luxe. Illustrated. From 1 50 up.

**FRANCIS DE SALES, ST.** Guide for Confession and Communion. Translated by Mrs. BENNETT-GLADSTONE. 32mo, 0 60
———— Maxims and Counsels for Every Day. 32mo, 0 50
———— New Year Greetings. 32mo, flexible cloth, 15 cents; per 100, 10 00

**GENERAL PRINCIPLES OF THE RELIGIOUS LIFE.** By Very Rev. BONIFACE F. VERHEYEN, O.S.B. 32mo, *net*, 0 30

**GLORIES OF DIVINE GRACE.** From the German of Dr. M. Jos. SCHEEBEN, by a BENEDICTINE MONK. 12mo, *net*, 1 50

**GLORIES OF MARY.** By St. Alphonsus. 2 vols. 12mo, *net*, 2 50

**GOD KNOWABLE AND KNOWN.** RONAYNE. 12mo, *net*, 1 25

**GOFFINE'S DEVOUT INSTRUCTIONS.** Illustrated Edition. Preface by His Eminence Cardinal GIBBONS. 8vo, cloth, 1.00; 10 copies, 7.50; 25 copies, 17.50; 50 copies, 33 50
  This is the best, the cheapest, and the most popular illustrated edition of Goffine's Instructions.

"GOLDEN SANDS," Books by the Author of:
  Golden Sands. Little Counsels for the Sanctification and Happiness of Daily Life. Third, Fourth, Fifth Series. 32mo, each, 0 60
  Book of the Professed. 32mo.
  Vol. I.  ⎫                                              *net*, 0 75
  Vol. II. ⎬  Each with a steel-plate Frontispiece.  *net*, 0 60
  Vol. III.⎭                                              *net*, 0 60
  Prayer. 32mo, *net*, 0 40
  The Little Book of Superiors. 32mo, *net*, 0 60
  Spiritual Direction. 32mo, *net*, 0 60
  Little Month of May. 32mo, flexible cloth, 0 25
  Little Month of the Poor Souls. 32mo, flexible cloth, 0 25
  Hints on Letter-Writing. 16mo, 0 60

GROU, REV. J., S.J. The Characteristics of True Devotion. A new edition, by Rev. SAMUEL H. FRISBEE, S.J. 16mo, *net*, 0 75

—— The Interior of Jesus and Mary. Edited by Rev. SAMUEL H. FRISBEE, S.J. 16mo, 2 vols., *net*, 2 00

HANDBOOK FOR ALTAR SOCIETIES, and Guide for Sacristans and others having charge of the Altar and Sanctuary. 16mo. *net*, 0 75

HANDBOOK OF THE CHRISTIAN RELIGION. By Rev. W. WILMERS, S.J. From the German. Edited by Rev. JAMES CONWAY, S.J. 12mo, *net*, 1 50

HAPPY YEAR, A; or, The Year Sanctified by Meditating on the Maxims and Sayings of the Saints. By ABBÉ LASAUSSE. 12mo, *net*, 1 00

HEART, THE, OF ST. JANE FRANCES DE CHANTAL. Thoughts and Prayers. 32mo, *net*, 0 40

HEIR OF DREAMS, AN. By SALLIE MARGARET O'MALLEY. 16mo, 0 50

HELP FOR THE POOR SOULS IN PURGATORY. Sm. 32mo, 0 50

HIDDEN TREASURE; or, The Value and Excellence of the Holy Mass. By ST. LEONARD OF PORT-MAURICE. 32mo, 0 50

HISTORY OF THE CATHOLIC CHURCH. By Dr. H. BRUECK. 2 vols., 8vo, *net*, 3 00

HISTORY OF THE CATHOLIC CHURCH. Adapted by Rev. RICHARD BRENNAN, LL.D. With 90 Illustrations. 8vo, 1 50

HISTORY OF THE MASS and its Ceremonies in the Eastern and Western Church. By Rev. JOHN O'BRIEN, A.M. 12mo, *net*, 1 25

HOLY FACE OF JESUS, THE. A Series of Meditations on the Litany of the Holy Face. 32mo, 0 50

HOURS BEFORE THE ALTAR; or, Meditations on the Holy Eucharist. By Mgr. DE LA BOUILLERIE. 32mo, 0 50

HOW TO GET ON. By Rev. BERNARD FEENEY. 12mo, 1 00

HOW TO MAKE THE MISSION. By a Dominican Father. 16mo, paper, 10 cents; per 100, 5 00

HUNOLT'S SERMONS. *Complete Unabridged Edition.* Translated from the original German edition of Cologne, 1740, by the Rev. J. ALLEN, D.D.   12 vols., 8vo,   30 00
Vols. 1, 2. The Christian State of Life.
Vols. 3, 4. The Bad Christian.
Vols. 5, 6. The Penitent Christian.
Vols. 7, 8. The Good Christian.
Vols. 9, 10. The Christian's Last End.
Vols. 11, 12. The Christian's Model.

His Eminence Cardinal Gibbons, Archbishop of Baltimore : " . . . Contain a fund of solid doctrine, presented in a clear and forcible style. These sermons should find a place in the library of every priest. . . ."

HUNOLT'S SHORT SERMONS. *Abridged Edition.* Arranged for all the Sundays of the year. 8vo, 5 vols.,   *net*, 10 00

IDOLS; or, The Secret of the Rue Chaussée d'Antin. A novel. By RAOUL DE NAVERY.  12mo,   1 25

ILLUSTRATED PRAYER-BOOK FOR CHILDREN. 32mo, 0 35

IMITATION OF THE BLESSED VIRGIN MARY. After the Model of the Imitation of Christ. Translated by Mrs. A. R. BENNETT-GLADSTONE. Small 32mo,   0 50
Edition de luxe, with fine illustrations. 32mo,   from 1 50 up.

INSTRUCTIONS ON THE COMMANDMENTS and the Sacraments. By ST. LIGUORI. 32mo. Paper, 0.25; per 100,   12 50
Cloth, 0.35; per 100,   21 00

KONINGS, THEOLOGIA MORALIS. Novissimi Ecclesiæ Doctoris S. Alphonsi. Editio septima, auctior, et novis curis expolitior, curante HENRICO KUPER, C.SS.R. Two vols. in one, half morocco,   *net*, 4 00

—— Commentarium in Facultates Apostolicas. New, greatly enlarged edition. 12mo,   *net*, 2 25

—— General Confession Made Easy. 32mo, flex.,   0 15

LAMP OF THE SANCTUARY. A tale. Wiseman. 48mo, 0 25

LEGENDS AND STORIES OF THE HOLY CHILD JESUS from Many Lands. Collected by A. FOWLER LUTZ. 16mo, 0 75

LEPER QUEEN, THE. A Story of the Thirteenth Century. 16mo,   0 50

LETTERS OF ST. ALPHONSUS LIGUORI. Centenary Edition. 5 vols., 12mo. Each,   *net*, 1 25

LIBRARY OF THE RELIGIOUS LIFE. Composed of "Book of the Professed," by the author of "Golden Sands," 3 vols. ; "Spiritual Direction," by the author of "Golden Sands"; and "Souvenir of the Novitiate." 5 vols., 32mo, in case,   3 25

LIFE AND ACTS OF LEO XIII. By Rev. JOSEPH E. KELLER, S.J. Fully and beautifully illustrated. 8vo,   2 00

LIFE OF ST. ALOYSIUS GONZAGA. Edited by Rev. F. GOLDIE, S.J. Edition de luxe, richly illustrated. 8vo,   *net*, 2 50

LIFE OF THE BLESSED VIRGIN, ILLUSTRATED. Adapted by Rev. RICHARD BRENNAN, LL.D. With fine half-tone illustrations. 12mo,   1 25

LIFE OF CHRIST, ILLUSTRATED. By Father M. v. Cochem. Adapted by Rev. B. Hammer, O.S.F. With fine half-tone illustrations. 12mo, 1 25

LIFE OF FATHER CHARLES SIRE. By his brother, Rev. Vital Sire. 12mo. *net*, 1 00

LIFE OF ST. CLARE OF MONTEFALCO. By Rev. Joseph A. Locke, O.S.A. 12mo, *net*, 0 75

LIFE OF THE VEN. MARY CRESCENTIA HÖSS. 12mo, *net*, 1 25

LIFE OF ST. FRANCIS SOLANUS. 16mo, *net*, 0 50

LIFE OF ST. GERMAINE COUSIN. 16mo, 0 50

LIFE OF ST. CHANTAL. See under St. Chantal. *net*, 4 00

(LIFE OF) MOST REV. JOHN HUGHES, First Archbishop of New York. By Rev. H. A. Brann, D.D. 12mo, *net*, 0 75

LIFE OF FATHER JOGUES. By Father Felix Martin, S.J. From the French by John Gilmary Shea. 12mo, *net*, 0 75

LIFE OF MLLE. LE GRAS. 12mo, *net*, 1 25

LIFE OF MARY FOR CHILDREN. By Anne R. Bennett, née Gladstone. 24mo, illustrated, *net*, 0 50

LIFE OF RIGHT REV. JOHN N. NEUMANN, D.D. By Rev. E. Grimm, C.SS.R. 12mo, *net*, 1 25

LIFE OF FR. FRANCIS POILVACHE. 32mo, paper, *net*, 0 20

LIFE OF OUR LORD AND SAVIOUR JESUS CHRIST and of His Blessed Mother. Adapted by Rev. Richard Brennan, LL.D. With nearly 600 illustrations. No. 1. cloth, *net*, 5 00
No. 3. Morocco back and corners, gilt edges, *net*, 7 00
No. 4. Full morocco, richly gilt back, gilt edges, *net*, 9 00
No. 5. Full morocco, block-panelled sides, gilt edges, *net*, 10 00

LIFE, POPULAR, OF ST. TERESA OF JESUS. By L'Abbé Marie-Joseph. 12mo, *net*, 0 75

LIGUORI, ST. ALPHONSUS DE. Complete Ascetical Works of. Centenary Edition. Edited by Rev. Eugene Grimm, C.SS.R. Price, per volume, *net*, 1 25

Each book is complete in itself, and any volume will be sold separately.

Preparation for Death.
Way of Salvation and of Perfection.
Great Means of Salvation and Perfection.
Incarnation, Birth, and Infancy of Christ.
The Passion and Death of Christ.
The Holy Eucharist.
The Glories of Mary, 2 vols.
Victories of the Martyrs.
True Spouse of Christ, 2 vols.
Dignity and Duties of the Priest.
The Holy Mass.
The Divine Office.
Preaching.
Abridged Sermons for all the Sundays.
Miscellany.
Letters, 4 vols.
Letters and General Index.

LINKED LIVES. A novel. By Lady Douglas. 8vo, 1 50

LITTLE CHILD OF MARY. Large 48mo, 0 25
LITTLE MANUAL OF ST. ANTHONY. Illustrated. 32mo, cloth, 0 60
LITTLE OFFICE OF THE IMMACULATE CONCEPTION. 32mo, paper, 3 cents; per 100, 2 00
LITTLE PICTORIAL LIVES OF THE SAINTS. With Reflections for Every Day in the Year. Edited by JOHN GILMARY SHEA, LL.D. With nearly 400 illustrations. 12mo, cloth, ink and gold side, 1 00
   10 copies, 6.25; 25 copies, 15.00; 50 copies, 27.50; 100 copies, 50 00
   This book has received the approbation of 30 Archbishops and Bishops.
LITTLE PRAYER-BOOK OF THE SACRED HEART. Prayers and Practices of Blessed Margaret Mary. Sm. 32mo, cloth, 0 40
LITTLE SAINT OF NINE YEARS. From the French of Mgr. DE SEGUR, by MARY MCMAHON. 16mo, 0 50
LOURDES. Its Inhabitants, Its Pilgrims, Its Miracles. By R. F. CLARKE, S.J. 16mo, illustrated, 0 75
LUTHER'S OWN STATEMENTS concerning his Teachings and its Results. By HENRY O'CONNOR, S.J. 12mo, paper, 0 15
MANIFESTATION OF CONSCIENCE. Confessions and Communions in Religious Communities. By Rev. PIE DE LANGOGNE, O.M.Cap. 32mo, *net*, 0 50
MANUAL OF THE HOLY EUCHARIST. Conferences and Pious Practices, with Devotions for Mass, etc. Prepared by Rev. F. X. Lasance, Director of the Tabernacle Society of Cincinnati. Oblong 24mo, 0 75
MANUAL OF THE HOLY FAMILY. Prayers and Instructions for Catholic Parents. 32mo, cloth, 0 60
MANUAL OF INDULGENCED PRAYERS. A Complete Prayer-Book. Arranged and disposed for daily use. Small 32mo, 0 40
MARCELLA GRACE. A novel. By ROSA MULHOLLAND. With illustrations after original drawings. 12mo, 1 25
MARRIAGE. By Very Rev. PÈRE MONSABRÉ, O.P. From the French, by M. HOPPER. 12mo, *net*, 1 00
MAY DEVOTIONS, NEW. Reflections on the Invocations of the Litany of Loretto. 12mo, *net*, 1 00
McCALLEN, REV. JAMES A., S.S. Sanctuary Boy's Illustrated Manual. 12mo, *net*, 0 50
—— Office of Tenebræ. 12mo, *net*, 1 00
—— Appendix. Containing Harmonizations of the Lamentations. 12mo, *net*, 0 75
MEANS OF GRACE, THE. A Complete Exposition of the Seven Sacraments, of the Sacramentals, and of Prayer, with a Comprehensive Explanation of the "Lord's Prayer" and the "Hail Mary." By Rev. RICHARD BRENNAN, LL.D. With 180 full-page and other illustrations. 8vo, cloth, 2.50; gilt edges, 3.00; Library edition, half levant, 3 50
MEDITATIONS (BAXTER) for Every Day in the Year. By Rev. ROGER BAXTER, S.J. Small 12mo, *net*, 1 25

MEDITATIONS (CHAIGNON, S.J.) FOR THE USE OF THE SECULAR CLERGY. By Father CHAIGNON, S.J. From the French, by Rt. Rev. L. DE GOESBRIAND, D.D. 2 vols., 8vo, *net*, 4 00

MEDITATIONS (HAMON'S) FOR ALL THE DAYS OF THE YEAR. For the use of Priests, Religious, and the Laity. By Rev. M. HAMON, SS., Pastor of St. Sulpice, Paris. From the French, by Mrs. ANNE R. BENNETT-GLADSTONE. With Alphabetic Index. 5 vols., 16mo, cloth, gilt top, each with a Steel Engraving. *net*, 5 00

"Hamon's doctrine is the unadulterated word of God, presented with unction, exquisite taste, and freed from that exaggerated and sickly sentimentalism which disgusts when it does not mislead."—MOST REV. P. L. CHAPELLE, D.D.

MEDITATIONS (PERINALDO) on the Sufferings of Jesus Christ. From the Italian of Rev. FRANCIS DA PERINALDO, O.S.F. 12mo, *net*, 0 75

MEDITATIONS (VERCRUYSSE), for Every Day in the Year, on the Life of Our Lord Jesus Christ. By the Rev. Father BRUNO VERCRUYSSE, S.J. 2 vols., *net*, 2 75

MEDITATIONS ON THE PASSION OF OUR LORD. By a PASSIONIST FATHER. 32mo, 0 40

MISSION BOOK of the Redemptorist Fathers. 32mo, cloth, 0 50

MISSION BOOK FOR THE MARRIED. By Very Rev. F. GIRARDEY, C.SS.R. 32mo, 0 50

MISSION BOOK FOR THE SINGLE. By Very Rev. F. GIRARDEY, C.SS.R. 32mo, 0 50

MISTRESS OF NOVICES, The, Instructed in her Duties. From the French of the ABBÉ LEGUAY, by Rev. IGNATIUS SISK. 12mo, cloth, *net*, 0 75

MOMENTS BEFORE THE TABERNACLE. By Rev. MATTHEW RUSSELL, S.J. 24mo, *net*, 0 40

MONK'S PARDON. A Historical Romance of the Time of Philip IV. of Spain. By RAOUL DE NAVERY. 12mo, 1 25

MONTH OF THE DEAD. 32mo, 0 75

MONTH OF MAY. From the French of Father DEBUSSI, S J., by ELLA MCMAHON. 32mo, 0 50

MONTH OF THE SACRED HEART. HUGUET. 0 75

MONTH, NEW, OF MARY, St. Francis de Sales. 32mo, 0 40

MONTH, NEW, OF THE SACRED HEART, St. Francis de Sales. 32mo, 0 40

MONTH, NEW, OF ST. JOSEPH, St. Francis de Sales. 32mo, 0 40

MONTH, NEW, OF THE HOLY ANGELS, St. Francis de Sales. 32mo, 0 40

MOOTED QUESTIONS OF HISTORY. By H. DESMOND. 16mo, 0 75

MR. BILLY BUTTONS. A novel. By WALTER LECKY. 12mo, 1 25

MY FIRST COMMUNION: The Happiest Day of My Life. BRENNAN. 16mo, illustrated, 0 75

MÜLLER, REV. MICHAEL, C.SS.R. God the Teacher of Mankind. A plain, comprehensive Explanation of Christian Doctrine. 9 vols., crown 8vo. Per set, *net*, 9 50
The Church and Her Enemies. *net*, 1 10
The Apostles' Creed. *net*, 1 10
The First and Greatest Commandment. *net*, 1 40
Explanation of the Commandments, continued. Precepts of the Church. *net*, 1 10
Dignity, Authority, and Duties of Parents, Ecclesiastical and Civil Powers. Their Enemies. *net*, 1 40
Grace and the Sacraments. *net*, 1 25
Holy Mass. *net*, 1 25
Eucharist and Penance. *net*, 1 10
Sacramentals—Prayer, etc. *net*, 1 00

—— Familiar Explanation of Catholic Doctrine. 12mo, 1 00

—— The Prodigal Son; or, The Sinner's Return to God. 8vo, *net*, 1 00

—— The Devotion of the Holy Rosary and the Five Scapulars. 8vo, *net*, 0 75

—— The Catholic Priesthood. 2 vols., 8vo, *net*, 3 00

NAMES THAT LIVE IN CATHOLIC HEARTS. By ANNA T. SADLIER. 12mo, 1 00

NEW TESTAMENT, THE. Illustrated Edition. With 100 fine full-page illustrations. Printed in two colors. 16mo, *net*, 0 60

The advantages of this edition over others consist in its beautiful illustrations, its convenient size, its clear, open type, and substantial and attractive binding. It is the best adapted for general use on account of its compactness and low price.

OFFICE, COMPLETE, OF HOLY WEEK, in Latin and English. 24mo, cloth, 0.50; cloth, limp, gilt edges, 1 00
Also in finer bindings.

O'GRADY, ELEANOR. Aids to Correct and Effective Elocution. 12mo, 1 25

—— Select Recitations for Schools and Academies. 12mo, 1 00

—— Readings and Recitations for Juniors. 16mo, *net*, 0 50

—— Elocution Class. 16mo, *net*, 0 50

ON CHRISTIAN ART. By EDITH HEALY. 16mo, 0 50

ON THE ROAD TO ROME, and How Two Brothers Got There. By WILLIAM RICHARDS. 16mo, 0 50

ONE AND THIRTY DAYS WITH BLESSED MARGARET MARY. 32mo, flexible cloth, 0 25

ONE ANGEL MORE IN HEAVEN. With Letters of Condolence by St. Francis de Sales and others. White mor., 0 50

OUR BIRTHDAY BOUQUET. Culled from the Shrines of Saints and the Gardens of Poets. By E. C. DONNELLY. 16mo, 1 00

OUR FAVORITE DEVOTIONS. By Very Rev. Dean A. A. LINGS. 24mo, 0 60

While there are many excellent books of devotion, there is none made on the plans of this one, giving ALL the devotions in general use among the faithful. It will be found a very serviceable book.

OUR FAVORITE NOVENAS. By the Very Rev. Dean A. A.
LINGS. 24mo, 0 60
Gives forms of prayer for all the novenas for the feasts of Our Lord, the Blessed Virgin, and the Saints which pious custom has established.

OUR LADY OF GOOD COUNSEL IN GENAZZANO. By
ANNE R. BENNETT, née GLADSTONE. 32mo, 0 75

OUR OWN WILL, and How to Detect it in our Actions. By Rev.
JOHN ALLEN, D.D. 16mo, *net*, 0 75

OUR YOUNG FOLKS' LIBRARY. 10 volumes. 12mo. Each,
0 45; per set, 3 00

OUTLAW OF CAMARGUE, THE. A novel. By A. DE LAMOTHE,
12mo, 1 25

OUTLINES OF DOGMATIC THEOLOGY. By Rev. SYLVESTER
J. HUNTER, S.J. 3 vols., 12mo, *net*, 4 50

PARADISE ON EARTH OPENED TO ALL; or, A Religious
Vocation the Surest Way in Life. 32mo, *net*, 0 40

PASSING SHADOWS. A novel. By ANTHONY YORKE. 12mo, 1 25

PEARLS FROM FABER. Selected and arranged by MARION J.
BRUNOWE. 32mo, 0 50

PETRONILLA, and other Stories. By E. C. DONNELLY. 12mo, 1 00

PHILOSOPHY, ENGLISH MANUALS OF CATHOLIC.
    Logic. By RICHARD F. CLARKE, S.J. 12mo, *net*, 1 25
    First Principles of Knowledge. By JOHN RICKABY, S.J.
    12mo, *net*, 1 25
    Moral Philosophy (Ethics and Natural Law). By JOSEPH
    RICKABY, S.J. 12mo, *net*, 1 25
    Natural Theology. By BERNARD BOEDDER, S.J. 12mo, *net*, 1 50
    Psychology. By MICHAEL MAHER, S.J. 12mo, *net*, 1 50
    General Metaphysics. By JOHN RICKABY, S.J. 12mo, *net*, 1 25
    Manual of Political Economy. By C. S. DEVAS. 12mo, *net*, 1 50

PEW-RENT RECEIPT BOOK. 800 receipts, *net*, 1 00

PICTORIAL LIVES OF THE SAINTS. With Reflections for
Every Day in the Year. 50th Thousand. 8vo, 2 00
5 copies, 6.65; 10 copies, 12.50; 25 copies, 27.50; 50 copies, 50 00

POPULAR INSTRUCTIONS ON MARRIAGE. By Very Rev.
F. GIRARDEY, C.SS.R. 32mo. Paper, 0.25; per 100, 12 50
Cloth, 0.35; per 100, 21 00

POPULAR INSTRUCTIONS TO PARENTS on the Bringing Up
of Children. By Very Rev. F. GIRARDEY, C.SS.R. 32mo.
Paper, 0.25; per 100, 12.50. Cloth, 0.35; per 100, 21 00

PRAYER. The Great Means of Obtaining Salvation. LIGUORI.
32mo, 0 50

PRAYER-BOOK FOR LENT. Meditations and Prayers for Lent.
32mo, cloth, 0 50

PRAXIS SYNODALIS. Manuale Synodi Diocesanæ ac Provincialis Celebrandæ. 12mo, *net*, 0 60

PRIEST IN THE PULPIT, THE. A Manual of Homiletics and
Catechetics. SCHUECH-LUEBBERMANN. 8vo, *net*, 1 50

PRIMER FOR CONVERTS, A. By Rev. J. T. DURWARD. 32mo,
flexible cloth, 0 25

PRINCIPLES OF ANTHROPOLOGY AND BIOLOGY. By Rev.
Thomas Hughes, S.J. 16mo, *net*, 0 75
REASONABLENESS OF CATHOLIC CEREMONIES AND
PRACTICES. By Rev. J. J. Burke. 12mo, flexible cloth, 0 35
READING AND THE MIND, WITH SOMETHING TO READ.
O'Conor, S.J. 12mo, *net*, 0 50
REGISTRUM BAPTISMORUM. 3,200 registers. 11 x 16
inches, *net*, 3 50
REGISTRUM MATRIMONIORUM. 3,200 registers. 11 x 16
inches, *net*, 3 50
RELIGIOUS STATE, THE. With a Short Treatise on Vocation
to the Priesthood. By St. Alphonsus Liguori. 32mo, 0 50
REMINISCENCES OF RT. REV. EDGAR P. WADHAMS, D.D.,
By Rev. C. A. Walworth. 12mo, illustrated, *net*, 1 00
RIGHTS OF OUR LITTLE ONES; or, First Principles of Education in Catechetical Form. By Rev. James Conway, S.J.
32mo, paper, 0.15; per 100, 9.00; cloth, 0.25; per 100, 15 00
ROSARY, THE MOST HOLY, in Thirty-one Meditations, Prayers,
and Examples. By Rev. Eugene Grimm, C.SS.R. 32mo, 0 50
ROUND TABLE, A, of the Representative *American* Catholic
Novelists, containing the best stories by the best writers. With
half-tone portraits, printed in colors, biographical sketches, etc.
12mo, 1 50
ROUND TABLE, A, of the Representative *Irish and English*
Catholic Novelists, containing the best stories by the best
writers. With half-tone portraits, printed in colors, biographical
sketches, etc. 12mo, 1 50
RUSSO, N., S.J.—De Philosophia Morali Prælectiones in Collegio
Georgiopolitano Soc. Jes. Anno 1889-1890 Habitæ, a Patre
Nicolao Russo. Editio altera. 8vo, half leather, *net*, 2 00
SACRAMENT OF PENANCE, THE. Lenten Sermons. Paper,
*net*, 0 25
SACRIFICE OF THE MASS WORTHILY CELEBRATED, THE.
By the Rev. Father Chaignon, S.J. Translated by Rt. Rev. L.
de Goesbriand, D.D. 8vo, *net*, 1 50
SACRISTY RITUAL. Rituale Compendiosum, seu Ordo Administrandi quædam Sacramenta et alia officia Ecclesiastica Rite peragendi ex Rituale Romano novissime edito desumptas. 16mo,
flexible, *net*, 0 75
ST. CHANTAL AND THE FOUNDATION OF THE VISITATION. By Monseigneur Bougaud. 2 vols., 8vo, *net*, 4 00
ST. JOSEPH OUR ADVOCATE. From the French of Rev. Father
Huguet. 24mo, 1 00
SACRAMENTALS OF THE HOLY CATHOLIC CHURCH,
THE. By Rev. A. A. Lambing, LL.D. Illustrated edition.
24mo.
Paper, 0.25; 25 copies, 4.25; 50 copies, 7.50; 100 copies, 12 50
Cloth, 0.50; 25 copies, 8.50; 50 copies, 15.00; 100 copies, 25 00

SACRED HEART, BOOKS ON THE.
    Child's Prayer-Book of the Sacred Heart. Small 32mo,   0 25
    Devotions to the Sacred Heart for the First Friday. 32mo, 0 40
    Imitation of the Sacred Heart of Jesus. By Rev. F. ARNOUDT, S.J.
        From the Latin by Rev. J. M. FASTRE, S.J. 16mo, cloth, 1 25
    Little Prayer-Book of the Sacred Heart. Small 32mo,   0 40
    Month of the Sacred Heart of Jesus. HUGUET. 32mo,   0 75
    Month of the Sacred Heart for the Young Christian. By
        BROTHER PHILIPPE. 32mo,   0 50
    New Month of the Sacred Heart, St. Francis de Sales. 32mo, 0 40
    One and Thirty Days with Blessed Margaret Mary. 32mo, 0 25
    Pearls from the Casket of the Sacred Heart of Jesus. 32mo, 0 50
    Revelations of the Sacred Heart to Blessed Margaret Mary;
        and the History of her Life. BOUGAUD. 8vo,   *net*, 1 50
    Sacred Heart Studied in the Sacred Scriptures. By Rev. H.
        SAINTRAIN, C.SS.R. 8vo,   *net*, 2 00
    Six Sermons on Devotion to the Sacred Heart of Jesus. BIER-
        BAUM. 16mo,   *net*, 0 60
    Year of the Sacred Heart. Drawn from the works of PÈRE DE
        LA COLOMBIÈRE, of Margaret Mary, and of others. 32mo, 0 50

SACRED RHETORIC. 12mo,   *net*, 0 75

SECRET OF SANCTITY, THE. According to ST. FRANCIS DE
    SALES and Father CRASSET, S.J. 12mo,   *net*, 1 00

SERAPHIC GUIDE. A Manual for the Members of the Third
    Order of St. Francis.   0 60
    Roan, red edges,   0 75
    The same in German at the same prices.

SERMONS. See also "Sacrament of Penance," "Seven Last
    Words," "Two-Edged Sword," and "Hunolt."

SERMONS, EIGHT SHORT PRACTICAL, ON MIXED MAR-
    RIAGES. By Rev. A. A. LAMBING, LL.D. Paper,   *net*, 0 25

SERMONS, OLD AND NEW. 8 vols., 8vo,   *net*, 16 00

SERMONS, LENTEN. Large 8vo,   *net*, 2 00

SERMONS, FUNERAL. 2 vols.,   *net*, 2 00

SERMONS ON THE CHRISTIAN VIRTUES. By the Rev. F.
    HUNOLT, S.J. Translated by Rev. J. ALLEN, D.D. 2 vols.,
    8vo,   *net*, 5 00

SERMONS ON THE DIFFERENT STATES OF LIFE. By Rev
    F. HUNOLT, S.J. Translated by Rev. J. ALLEN, D.D. 2 vols.,
    8vo,   *net*, 5 0c

SERMONS ON THE SEVEN DEADLY SINS. By Rev. F.
    HUNOLT, S.J. Translated by Rev. J. ALLEN, D.D. 2 vols.,
    8vo.,   *net*, 5 00

SERMONS ON PENANCE. By Rev. F. HUNOLT, S.J. Translated
    by Rev. J. ALLEN, D.D. 2 vols., 8vo,   *net*, 5 00

SERMONS ON OUR LORD, THE BLESSED VIRGIN, AND THE SAINTS. By Rev. F. HUNOLT, S.J. Translated by Rev. J. ALLEN, D.D. 2 vols., 8vo, *net*, 5 00

SERMONS ON THE BLESSED VIRGIN. By Very Rev. D. I. MCDERMOTT. 16mo, *net*, o 75

SERMONS, abridged, for all the Sundays and Holydays. By ST. ALPHONSUS LIGUORI. 12mo, *net*, 1 25

SERMONS for the Sundays and Chief Festivals of the Ecclesiastical Year. With Two Courses of Lenten Sermons and a Triduum for the Forty Hours. By Rev. JULIUS POTTGEISSER, S.J. From the German by Rev. JAMES CONWAY, S.J. 2 vols., 8vo, *net*, 2 50

SERMONS ON THE MOST HOLY ROSARY. By Rev. M. J. FRINGS. 12mo, *net*, 1 00

SERMONS, SHORT, FOR LOW MASSES. A complete, brief course of instruction on Christian Doctrine. By Rev. F. X. SCHOUPPE, S.J. 12mo, *net*, 1 25

SERMONS, SIX, on Devotion to the Sacred Heart of Jesus. From the German of Rev. Dr. E. BIERBAUM, by ELLA MCMAHON, 16mo, *net*, o 60

SEVEN LAST WORDS ON THE CROSS. Sermons. Paper, *net*, o 25

SHORT CONFERENCES ON THE LITTLE OFFICE OF THE IMMACULATE CONCEPTION. By Very Rev. JOSEPH RAINER. With Prayers. 32mo, o 50

SHORT STORIES ON CHRISTIAN DOCTRINE: A Collection of Examples Illustrating the Catechism. From the French by MARY MCMAHON. 12mo, illustrated, *net*, o 75

SMITH, Rev. S. B., D.D. Elements of Ecclesiastical Law.
    Vol. I. Ecclesiastical Persons. 8vo, *net*, 2 50
    Vol. II. Ecclesiastical Trials. 8vo, *net*, 2 50
    Vol. III. Ecclesiastical Punishments. 8vo, *net*, 2 50
——— Compendium Juris Canonici, ad Usum Cleri et Seminariorum hujus regionis accommodatum. 8vo, *net*, 2 00
——— The Marriage Process in the United States. 8vo, *net*, 2 50

SODALISTS' VADE MECUM. A Manual, Prayer-Book, and Hymnal. 32mo, cloth, o 50

SOUVENIR OF THE NOVITIATE. From the French by Rev. EDWARD I. TAYLOR. 32mo, *net*, o 60

SPIRITUAL CRUMBS FOR HUNGRY LITTLE SOULS. To which are added Stories from the Bible. RICHARDSON. 16mo, o 50

STANG, Rev. WILLIAM, D.D. Pastoral Theology. New enlarged edition. 8vo, *net*, 1 50
——— Eve of the Reformation. 12mo, paper, *net*, o 50

STORIES FOR FIRST COMMUNICANTS, for the Time before and after First Communion. By Rev. J. A. KELLER, D.D. 32mo, o 50

SUMMER AT WOODVILLE, A. By ANNA T. SADLIER. 16mo, o 50

SURE WAY TO A HAPPY MARRIAGE. A Book of Instructions for those Betrothed and for Married People. From the German by Rev. EDWARD I. TAYLOR. Paper, 0.25; per 100, 12.50; cloth, 0.35; per 100, 21 00

TALES AND LEGENDS OF THE MIDDLE AGES. From the Spanish of F. DE P. CAPELLA. By HENRY WILSON. 16mo, 0 75

TAMING OF POLLY, THE. By ELLA LORAINE DORSEY. 12mo, 0 85

TANQUEREY, Rev. Ad., S.S. Synopsis Theologiæ Fundamentalis. 8vo, *net*, 1 50

——— Synopsis Theologia Dogmatica Specialis. 2 vols., 8vo, *net*, 3 00

THINK WELL ON'T; or, Reflections on the Great Truths of the Christian Religion. By the Right Rev. R. CHALLONER, D.D. 32mo, flexible cloth, 0 20

THOUGHT FROM ST. ALPHONSUS, for Every Day of the Year. 32mo, 0 50

THOUGHT FROM BENEDICTINE SAINTS. 32mo, 0 50

THOUGHT FROM DOMINICAN SAINTS. 32mo, 0 50

THOUGHT FROM ST. FRANCIS ASSISI and his Saints. 32mo, 0 50

THOUGHT FROM ST. IGNATIUS. 32mo, 0 50

THOUGHT FROM ST. TERESA. 32mo, 0 50

THOUGHT FROM ST. VINCENT DE PAUL. 32mo, 0 50

THOUGHTS AND COUNSELS FOR THE CONSIDERATION OF CATHOLIC YOUNG MEN. By Rev. P. A. VON DOSS, S.J. 12mo, *net*, 1 25

THREE GIRLS AND ESPECIALLY ONE. By MARION AMES TAGGART. 16mo, 0 50

TRUE POLITENESS. Addressed to Religious. By Rev. FRANCIS DEMARE. 16mo, *net*, 0 60

TRUE SPOUSE OF CHRIST. By ST. ALPHONSUS LIGUORI. 2 vols., 12mo, *net*, 2.50; 1 vol., 12mo, 1 50

TWELVE VIRTUES, THE, of a Good Teacher. For Mothers, Instructors, etc. By Rev. H. POTTIER, S.J. 32mo, *net*, 0 30

TWO-EDGED SWORD, THE. Lenten Sermons. Paper. *net*, 0 25

TWO RETREATS FOR SISTERS. By Rev. E. ZOLLNER. 12mo, *net*, 1 00

VADE MECUM SACERDOTUM. Continens Preces ante et post Missam modum providendi Infirmos nec non multas Benedictionum Formulas. 48mo, cloth, *net*, 0.25; morocco, flexible, *net*, 0 50

VISIT TO EUROPE AND THE HOLY LAND. By Rev. H. F. FAIRBANKS. 12mo, illustrated, 1 50

VISITS TO THE MOST HOLY SACRAMENT and to the Blessed Virgin Mary. For Every Day of the Month. By ST. ALPHONSUS DE LIGUORI. Edited by Rev. EUGENE GRIMM. 32mo, 0 50

VOCATIONS EXPLAINED: Matrimony, Virginity, the Religious State, and the Priesthood. By a Vincentian Father. 16mo, flexible, 10 cents; per 100, 5 00
WARD, REV. THOS. F. Fifty-two Instructions on the Principal Truths of Our Holy Religion. 12mo, *net*, 0 75
—— Thirty-two Instructions for the Month of May and for the Feasts of the Blessed Virgin. 12mo, *net*, 0 75
—— Month of May at Mary's Altar. 12mo, *net*, 0 75
—— Short Instructions for all the Sundays and Holydays. 12mo, *net*, 1 25
WAY OF INTERIOR PEACE. By Rev. Father DE LEHEN, S.J. From the German Version of Rev. J. BRUCKER, S.J. 12mo, *net*, 1 25
WAY OF THE CROSS. Illustrated. Paper, 5 cents; per 100, 3 00
WHAT CATHOLICS HAVE DONE FOR SCIENCE, with Sketches of the Great Catholic Scientists. By Rev. MARTIN S. BRENNAN. 12mo, 1 00
WOMAN OF FORTUNE, A. A novel. By CHRISTIAN REID. 12mo, 1 25
WOMEN OF CATHOLICITY: Margaret O'Carroll—Isabella of Castile—Margaret Roper—Marie de l'Incarnation—Margaret Bourgeoys—Ethan Allen's Daughter. By ANNA T. SADLIER. 12mo, 1 00
WORDS OF JESUS CHRIST DURING HIS PASSION, Explained in their Literal and Moral Sense. By Rev. F. X. SCHOUPPE, S.J. Flexible cloth, 0 25
WORDS OF WISDOM. A Concordance of the Sapiential Books. 12mo, *net*, 1 25
WUEST, REV. JOSEPH, C.SS.R. DEVOTIO QUADRAGINTA HORARUM. 32mo, *net*, 0 25
YOUNG GIRL'S BOOK OF PIETY. 16mo, 1 00
ZEAL IN THE WORK OF THE MINISTRY; or, The Means by which every Priest may render his Ministry Honorable and Fruitful. From the French of L'ABBÉ DUBOIS. 8vo, *net*, 1 50

---

AN AMERICAN INDUSTRY. A full description of the Silversmith's Art and Ecclesiastical Metalwork as carried on in Benziger Brothers' Factory of Church Goods, De Kalb Avenue and Rockwell Place, Brooklyn, N. Y. Small quarto, 48 pp., with 75 illustrations, printed in two colors. Mailed gratis on application.

This interesting book gives a full description of the various arts employed in the manufacture of Church goods, from the designing and modelling, through the different branches of casting, spinning, chasing, buffing, gilding, and burnishing. The numerous beautiful half-tone illustrations show the machinery and tools used, as well as rich specimens of the work turned out.

www.ingramcontent.com/pod-product-compliance
Lightning Source LLC
Chambersburg PA
CBHW022113160426
43197CB00009B/1005